THE **PENGUIN RAY** LIBRARY

SATYAJIT RAY

Miscellany

On Life, Cinema, People & Much More

Edited by Sandip Ray

Co-edited by Riddhi Goswami
with additional editorial inputs by Debasis Mukhopadhyay

Layout and design by Pinaki De

THE **PENGUIN RAY** LIBRARY

PENGUIN BOOKS

USA | Canada | UK | Ireland | Australia
New Zealand | India | South Africa | China

Penguin Books is part of the Penguin Random House group of companies
whose addresses can be found at global.penguinrandomhouse.com

Published by Penguin Random House India Pvt. Ltd
4th Floor, Capital Tower 1, MG Road,
Gurugram 122 002, Haryana, India

First published in Penguin Books by Penguin Random House India 2022
In association with the Society for the Preservation of Satyajit Ray Archives

Copyright © Sandip Ray 2022

Vector illustration of Satyajit Ray's portrait on half-title page by Pinaki De

ISBN 9780143448990

Cover design and book layout by Pinaki De
Cover photograph by Nemai Ghosh courtesy Satyaki Ghosh
Printed at Thomson Press India Ltd, New Delhi

www.penguin.co.in

CONTENTS

PERSONAL NOTES

REMINISCENCES

FESTIVAL GREETINGS

LP SLEEVE NOTES

MISCELLANEOUS WRITINGS

Photograph by Sandip Ray

FOREWORD

Since his schooldays, my father was a cinema addict in the true sense of the term — lapping up Hollywood movies of Billy Wilder, William Wyler, Frank Capra and others as well as the timeless comedies of Chaplin and Keaton. The hobby gradually turned into a serious interest. The formation of the Calcutta Film Society in 1947 with a few like-minded friends opened to him the diverse range of European cinema, and in a sense, acted as a catalyst to his writings on cinema. In his first two articles, he heavily criticized the make-believe stereotypes of erstwhile Bengali cinema and called for soul-searching among the film-makers. The result — as he himself remarked later amusingly — "Nothing of that sort happened. The piece was simply shrugged off by the people of the trade as yet another piece of tomfoolery by some arrogant upstart who saw only foreign films and knew nothing of local needs and local conditions."

Later on, when he became a celebrated film-maker, there were always requests for articles from film club journals, newspapers and periodicals for their annual numbers.

Photograph by Pinaki De

Although by that time father was extremely busy with his two major pursuits — film-making and writing children's fiction — he always found time to pen down his thoughts. In his own words, "The reason why I keep writing about films from time to time is that perhaps at the back of my mind there are still remnants of the zeal to spread the film culture that brought our film club into being." Thus, we get a surprisingly myriad array of writings over the years; spanning film criticisms, reflections on silent cinema, and eminent film personalities, festival musings and snippets of greetings for film festivals and retrospectives. Time and again he reminisced about people he admired and loved. He also generously wrote introductions to other people's works — books on film, photography, painting, translations, LP music records — which bear testimony to his reverence towards the exponents of these diverse art forms.

The Penguin Ray Library is a great step to curate important works of the master so that they are easily accessible under one roof. I am immensely thankful to Premanka Goswami, associate publisher, Penguin Random House India, for his unabated support throughout the gestation of the project. Thanks are also due to the film journal *Chitravas* for collating many of the rare and elusive pieces.

It is really difficult to comment objectively about the work of a person whom you knew so closely. Still, as I look back, I feel that the discernable feature of all his writings has been his clarity of thought, sense of humour and economy of expression; which coupled with a sensitive mind, make these pieces extremely insightful forays into the thoughts of a true humanist auteur of the twenty-first century. While work for this volume was on, we were lucky to unearth some of his unpublished writings, rare photographs and manuscripts, all of which, I hope, will make this anthology a cherished volume for Satyajit Ray aficionados all over the world.

Sandip Ray

1/1 Bishop Lefroy Road,
Kolkata 700 020
May 2022

in 1940

1) Educated in Calcutta. Graduated from the Presidency College with Hons in Econ.
Studied painting for two/three years in Tagore's University at Santiniketan

Joined ~~as~~ a British advertising agency in 1943 as a Layout artist.
considerable free lance, work as typographer, book designer, Earn-up advertising from Held position of Art Director from '50 to '55. Rose up advertising
to ~~take up~~ ~~Vice~~ ~~Head~~ ~~Art~~ ~~Pather Panchali~~ ~~in ~~ ~~places~~ 1953-55 —
Started in 1953, finished it in 1955,
Shot Pather Panchali in ~~1954~~ shooting on Impulse, on Sundays & holidays.

2) No formal training in film making. Interested in movies since schooldays
in the beginning ~~point~~ generally
particularly the developing
~~point on a film fan~~ – there, ~~from about 44~~ instinct

into a Serious student ~~of cinema~~. Read practically all available
English books in English —. the usual Theorist – Pudovkin, Arnheim, Eisenstein,
Doto Spottiswoode. Learnt mainly from watching films – mostly Developed
Lubitsch too
American. of Directors like Ford, Capra, Wyler, Wilder, Huston, learnt
Our attached to
told than what in the theatre in the dark. Later on struck by book of
simplicity of American film
Renoir in Hollywood Deeply moved by Renoir's Southerner,

Later, on a visit to London, saw. Bicycle Thieves,

3) No specific category of film medium. Would take up any theme story
if sufficiently worth that felt strongly about. Make films
for primarily for the creative fun of it, but cannot entirely
Ignore business as but at back is the hope that a great
many enough should care for it to make investment
financially worthwhile. Feel humble to banish thought
consideration for the individual who provides cash important.
No desire to make esoteric films unless able to provide
finance myself. But strongly believe in healthy
films important should be healthy. Humanist. Dignity
mobility & sustainability.

Facsimile of the draft where Ray describes his journey as a film-maker

SATYAJIT RAY
A SELF-PORTRAIT

Sourced from Ray's notebook from an unfinished draft, c. 1960, previously unpublished.
Ray uses short truncated sentences to describe his journey as a film-maker.

The photograph used for Ray's first passport

Ray (right) working at D.J. Keymer, the British advertising agency

Educated in Calcutta. Graduated in 1940 from Presidency College with Honours in Economics. Studied painting for two–three years in Tagore's university at Santiniketan.

Joined a British advertising agency in 1943 as a layout artist. Continued freelance work as typographer and book illustrator. Held position of art director from 1950 to 1955. Started making *Pather Panchali* in 1953, finished it in 1955, shooting largely on Sundays and holidays.

Ray during his London visit, 1950

No formal training in film-making. Interested in movies since schooldays as a film fan — gradually developing a serious interest. Read all available books in English — the usual theorists — Pudovkin, Arnheim, Eisenstein, Spottiswoode. Learnt mainly from watching films — mostly American — of directors like Ford, Capra, Lubitsch, Wyler, Wilder, Houston. Developed own shorthand to take down notes in the theatre in the dark. Deeply moved by the simplicity of Renoir's American film, *The Southerner*. Later, on a visit to London, saw *Bicycle Thieves*.

No definite concepts or dogmas about the film medium. Would take up any theme that felt strongly about. Make films primarily for the creative part of it, but at back is the hope that enough should come for it to make commitment financially worthwhile. Feel consideration for the individual who provides cash important. No desire to make esoteric or avant-garde films unless able to finance myself. But strongly believe films should be healthy, humanist. Dislikes morbidity and sentimentality.

All my films have been based on existing stories to which I have felt strongly sympathetic. The choice is dictated as much by their themes as by their abstract filmic qualities. Invariably, in each case, the author's viewpoint has been modified and coloured by my own, in addition to the obvious transformations in the process of translation from one art form to another. Even before *Pather Panchali*, I had written scenarios for my own pleasure, mainly taking up stories which had been announced for production. This gave me an opportunity to compare my own treatment with the director's, often with unfortunate results. *Pather Panchali* seemed to have certain possibilities for an artistic film (by which I mean a film with abstract formal qualities), for its simplicity and humanity, which is the reason the same film has a wide range of appeal. I was also struck by its profundity, its lyricism and brimming honesty.

I tried to peddle the scenario for more than a year and visited every financier, producer and distributor in the city. At length we pushed our resources, obtained a loan against my insurance policies and launched the production. I had a job in an advertising agency at that time, and I had to keep it, because I invested part of my earnings to go into the production. Shooting, therefore, had to be confined largely to Sundays and holidays. Our funds ran out after two months. A distributor was then persuaded to advance about $4000, with which for some more shooting continued, but the results intimidated them and they backed out without any further contribution. At this point, some of my wife's jewellery

Ray during the music recording of *Pather Panchali*

went to the pawnshop and I had to part with most of my art books and classical records (phonographs). But shooting came to a standstill soon after this and there was no work for more than a year. I had decided to give up the production — it was hard to keep up the morale of the crew — when the West Bengal Government was persuaded to finance the film. A contract was drawn up and the Government acquired the property of the film, provided funds in small instalments until completion.

I really learnt film technique during the making of *Pather Panchali* and the very lesson I learnt was that it is one thing to theorize about film-making and quite another to make a film. The first six or seven days' footage was so shoddy that they all had to be reshot later on. My cameraman was new too, but quickly gained confidence. I have had the same crew in all my films.

I am not attracted by a story unless it simultaneously possesses two qualities: i) a theme, or a plot, or some characters, or situations, or at best, a combination of all, that will engage my full sympathy and interest; ii) it lends itself to treatment in terms of the cinema.

Pather Panchali was shot mostly outdoors with two or three different types of camera, all rented from studios. For the night scenes we hired floor spaces and built sets. At present we hire studio space for scenes that require sets. For outdoor shooting we have a camera of our own. The three trilogy films consisted mostly of non-professionals. But I have no prejudice against professionals and used many of them in my three other films. I generally have a fairly clear idea of what a particular character should be like. When a professional conforms to my requirement, I cast him. Otherwise I am obliged to look around for a non-professional.

I don't know how or if my technique differs from other directors, Indian or European. But this is how I generally go about making a film. Once I have decided on the story, I prepare a treatment. For this purpose, I generally go away to a quiet seaside resort, and in about a week's time the treatment is ready. This takes the form of a long synopsis which reads like a story. The main sequences are indicated and the dialogue is only touched on. This is good enough to provide a basis for casting and a breakdown in terms of sets and performers. There is no shooting script at any stage of

Sketch of Gopalpur-on-sea by Ray during one of his sojourns

the production. I write the dialogues as the film progresses, and the actors are provided with the lines at least three days before shooting. I keep the rehearsals to a minimum and keep brushing it until the very last moment. The scenes are broken down into shots a day before shooting (this leaves room for last-minute inspirations). The shots are sketched out in a book, which facilitates discussion with the cameraman and my assistants.

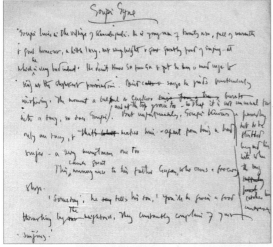

An example of a synopsis from Ray's notebook

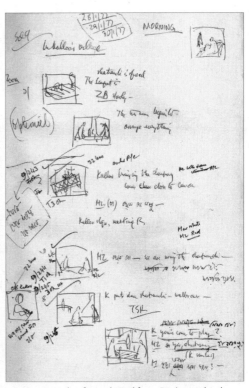

An example of storyboard from Ray's notebook

As for the actual shooting, I rehearse thoroughly only if it's a long take with a lot of dialogue. Otherwise a little preliminary discussion with the actors (no discussion at all if it's a child actor, where I merely ask them to do or say certain things in a certain manner without bothering them too much with the reason for saying or doing so), a couple of rehearsals and then take — seldom more than three — I *don't* cover a scene from all possible set-ups.

Ray during the shooting of *Sonar Kella* at Jaisalmer, 1973. Photograph by Sandip Ray

A DIRECTOR'S
PERSPECTIVE

Ray during the music recording of *Aparajito*, 1956

THE OUTLOOK FOR BENGALI FILMS

Published in *The Calcutta Municipal Gazette*, 8 March 1952

It is generally conceded that the film industry in Bengali is facing a big crisis. Some have gone so far as to predict a total annihilation of the Bengali film as such, and the sprouting up in its place of a product not dissimilar to the well-known type created by Bombay. This may be the height of pessimism, but there is no denying some alarming symptoms. Firstly, the area of exploitation of the Bengali film has been considerably reduced by the Partition; secondly, for reasons we shall presently examine, the exhibitors in Bengal have grown increasingly distrustful of the home product preferring the unpretentious, brassy and frankly escapist products of Bombay and more recently, Madras. To add to the general alarm, some of our ablest directors and technicians have left for more lucrative employment in Bombay and Madras.

AESTHETIC ASPECT

But although the pressure of circumstances has a great deal to do with the present predicament, it would be wrong to overlook the other aspect of — as well as a contributing factor to — the crisis. I refer to the aesthetic aspect. In the thirty years of its existence the Bengali film as a whole has not progressed one step towards maturity. Looking over the past three or four years one comes across a handful of commendable efforts — *Barjatri, Paribartan, Kabi, Ratnadeep, Vidyasagar, Swayamsiddhawa, Mantramugdha, Bhuli Nai,*

42, *Babla*, *Ramer Sumati*, *Pandit Mashai* and a few others — a bare dozen altogether, none entirely successful and satisfactory but each containing passages of acting, direction, writing or photography which if sustained would make for respectable cinema. As for the others (the overwhelming majority), they bear the same relation to art as they do the lithographs in Wellington Square to the art of painting or the "Mohan Series" to literature. These films neither stimulate the sensibilities nor please the senses. It may be argued that in any creative medium, greatness is the exception rather than the rule; that a good deal of painted and printed stuff that passes for painting and literature deserves to go down the drain. But whereas we have the Rabindranaths and the Nandalals to atone for the trivial and the dross, have we any comparable figure in our cinema? The answer must regretfully be in the negative. And there is a reason for it. The cinema, unquestionably the most complex and difficult of all the creative arts, has not been taken seriously enough by its practitioners. There is no director in Bengal whose work even momentarily suggests a total grasp of the film medium in its dramatic, plastic and literary aspects.

Some of our directors, such as Nitin Bose and the late Pramathesh Barua, have achieved technical excellence enlivened by occasional imaginative touches. But both have been too much under the influence of the American style and failed to achieve a genuinely national idiom. Debaki Bose, with his predilection for romantic national themes (*Vidyapati*, *Chandidas*, *Kabi*), has succeeded on occasions in imparting a genuine Indian flavour. But a lack of formal discipline (a besetting sin of every Indian director), an excessive fondness for outmoded literary symbolism (two pigeons: love), have robbed his films of tension and continuing interest and made them in the final analysis unsatisfying. Of recent directors, Hemen Gupta in *42* and *Bhuli Nai* has revealed genuine talent. The best moments of his film are also the best achievements of the Bengali cinema. One reason for this is his first-hand knowledge of the characters he portrays. But unfortunately, the pamphleteer and the platform-speaker element in Hemen Gupta frequently gets the better of him and an embarrassing overdose of sentimental nationalist speechifying frequently upsets the balance of his films. Satyen Bose is a promising director who has been very prudent with his material. His best film, *Barjatri*, had one of the finest ready-made scripts — the short stories of Bibhutibhushan Mukhopadhyay, rich in incident and details of observation — the very stuff of good cinema.

THE SCENARIO

This brings us to the all important basis of a good film — the scenario. In our country, in nine cases out of ten, the scenario is non-existent. There is some sort of dossier with some dialogue in it but most of the creative work takes place in the set on the spur of the moment. When it is a novel that is being filmed, one of two things usually happens. The director is either likely to make a slavish transcription of literary originals (as has been the case with most Sarat Chandra stories) which — unlike the original itself, is possessed of cinematic qualities of action and movements (as in *Barjatri*) — is not likely to result in good cinema. Alternately, if the scenarist himself is a writer in his own right he is likely to embellish the original with his own literary flourishes, often twisting the plot to suit his private whims and even in extreme cases to alter the names of the principal characters. As a classic instance of a twisted uncinematic version of a brilliant cinematic original, I would mention the Sajani Das-Nitin Bose version of Rabindranath's *Drishtidan*.

An inexplicable phenomenon in Bengali films has been the peculiarly unsatisfactory contribution of some of our best writers in the capacity of film directors. With an enormous preconception of the nature and function of films, these writers (the most important being Premendra Mitra and Sailajananda Mukhopadhyaya) have neglected the excellent cinematic material in their own writings — material with a genuine Bengali flavour — and preferred to go in for the most hybrid concoctions. Another writer preparing the scenario for his excellent filmic short story — *Fossil* — inflated and transmogrified it beyond recognition. The contemporary scene, the texture of city life, the drama of everyday existence have been shamefully neglected by our film-makers. Only one director, Jyotirmoy Roy, deserves the credit for tackling the problems of our day in a series of films beginning with *Udayar Pathe*, but the success of this first film (directed by Bimal Roy) has not been repeated because Jyotirmoy Roy's directional abilities are severely restricted and his too frequent verbal quips and repartees belong more to the late nineteenth-century stage than to the cinema of today.

MEND, OR END

The plain fact is: our directors have not yet learned the language of the cinema. This language, as we know, is primarily visual. In it, the settings and the atmosphere are at least as important as the characters; and the actions, more important than the words. How does one learn this language? Primarily, by observation, by keeping one's eyes as well as one's ears open which, incidentally, is also the primary requisite for a good novelist. A director is indeed like a novelist having the vocabulary of images and sounds instead of written words. But more than the novelist, the director needs to be economical and terse in his expansion. The time factor to him is enormously important. Nothing — not a scene, not a word, not a gesture — that is not directly contributive to the theme should find a place in that film, in the scenario. This discipline is not only conducive to better art, it is also likely to reduce the cost of film-making. The first step towards a reform — for a reform is badly, imperatively needed to salvage our industry — would be towards a simplification: simplification of story, of technique, of presentation. The next step would be to acquire a precise notion of what the director wants to say. How he wants to say it, will then follow naturally. Technical preoccupation is useless; one knows exactly what one is driving at. It must be realized that we have the technical resources to produce great films (the Italians have made masterpieces with less equipment). As for themes there is no end to them if one has the power to observe and select. And the public? Do they present a problem? I think not. The public responds to anything that gives them their money's worth — whether it be in the form of aesthetic stimulation or the satisfaction of their natural appetite for the romantic and the fantastic, or just plain escapist entertainment. It is only when all their natural expectations are denied that they turn back and protest. And unless a reform takes place quickly, they are likely to protest more and more and more — and hasten the end of the Bengali cinema.

A NEW APPROACH

Published in *Filmfare*, 17 August 1956

I think it can be stated as a general rule that the main incentive which keeps a director going with his job on a film is the hope that a great many people will pay to see the finished product and like it. In other words, he expects to make a hit and is goaded by the expectation.

That is as it should be.

Deliberately to set out to make a film for a small coterie may be all right where small private funds are involved: an avant-garde experiment in 16 mm, for instance.

But a director who is obliged to stick to normal production and distribution methods is also obliged to take into account the receptive capacities of the many rather than a few.

I was aware of this fact when I set out to make *Pather Panchali*, but the prospect did not discourage me. I had my own ideas of what makes a popular film which did not, as it happened, run counter to my ideas of what makes a good film.

These ideas may well be wrong. The wide range of appeal of *Pather Panchali* may be due to reasons entirely different from what I told them to be. But I would like to state them for what they are worth, and in the hope that contradictions may be forthcoming to further confuse the question of what makes a film click at the box office.

I have been credited with tackling a daring, undramatic, "documentary" (synonymous with "dry" I suppose) subject, and getting away with it.

Nothing could be farther from the truth.

Shooting of *Pather Panchali* in progress

Pather Panchali was my first film, and I chose it because I was convinced that it was a "safe" subject — among the safest in all Bengali literature. I was also convinced that it was dramatic subject, dramatic from the point of view of the screen and not the stage.

It is true that *Pather Panchali* had no clear-cut plot. But then, I do not believe that a film needs a clear-cut plot. What it needs, basically, is a theme, an idea, even a situation, perhaps a character, or a set of characters, which admits of most effective development in terms of visual images.

Pather Panchali had such a theme, a poignant human one, conveyed with all the truth and profundity that the great writer Bibhutibhushan Bandopadhyay was capable of. The human relationship the film depicts is of a dynamic nature. It makes possible dramatic development and interplay of characteristization in the course of the narrative. Let me say at once that this interplay, this drama, is not pronounced, but subtle. Nevertheless, it is truly cinematic and, being human, it is also effective.

The background of rural Bengal was also dynamic in its changing aspects from day to day and season to season. Bibhutibhushan had made the background an integral part of his theme, which considerably heightened its cinematic possibilities.

There was besides the important quality of contrast. Contrasts of mood, of texture, of pace; contrast of seasons; sunlight and shadow; sound and silence. Contrast between the beauty of the countryside and the sordidness of poverty; contrast between the children rejoicing in the meadows and the forest paths and the adults, frustrated and fatalistic, battling feebly and sporadically against hard circumstances.

Finally, but most important, the details. With his sensitive observation, Bibhutibhushan had ornamented his theme with a profusion of telling and truthful details, exciting in their possibilities of visual interpretation. I had a gold mine of film material in *Pather Panchali*.

Next came the question of approach, of finding the right cinematic style to suit the theme. The style of the original was a wonderful blend of realism and lyricism, and I was never in doubt that I had to strive for a cinematic equivalent of it.

Visual authenticity was of the utmost importance. The characters were real, with no hint of idealization, and they had therefore to perform against real backgrounds. This was no fad or dogma, but an absolute stylistic necessity so far as this film was concerned. I also felt that it was worth trying to get "atmosphere" into the film at any cost, because I believed it would heighten the drama. The subtle shades of difference between dawn and dusk, the dramatic qualities of the hot midday sun, the grey humid stillness that precedes the first monsoon shower — all these had somehow to be caught and conveyed.

This involved a respect for natural "available" light to an extent which sometimes created tough problems for the cameraman. But undaunted, we shot nearly all the scenes on location, and as far as possible in the time of the day and season in which they were supposed to have taken place in the story.

For instance, the girl falls ill at the onset of the monsoon, and all scenes following this episode were shot on dull cloudy days, at the expense perhaps of what is known as "pictorialism" in photography, but to the enormous gain of the overall mood. I am convinced of this gain.

Ray directing Chunibala Devi in *Pather Panchali*

The choice of new faces was also dictated by the anxiety to create believable characters. Established stars, with all due respect to them, tend to destroy the illusion of authenticity, unless they are sincere enough to shed all their well-known and wellloved mannerisms and identify themselves with the characters they are portraying. This happens only rarely, and I was happy to have a large non-professional cast.

All this meant hard work. Hard work for actors and technicians alike. We did not adopt shortcut methods, because we did not know of any. And I have a feeling, which borders on conviction, that if we had adopted them, *Pather Panchali* would not have won the success that it has.

Ray directing Karuna Banerjee in *Pather Panchali*

THOUGHTS ON FILM-MAKING

Previously unpublished. Unfinished article transcribed from the notebook of *Aparajito* (c. 1956)

I have so far made two films. The comments raised by them in writing and otherwise, particularly the latter — have been varied and instructive. Now that the critics — and I do not mean only the professional sort — have had their say, perhaps the artist may be permitted his point of view.

The main criticism levelled against *Aparajito* has been in the matter of deviations from the original novel. I should have thought that with the examples of filmed Shakespeare and filmed Dickens, the issue of adapting voluminous works for the screen has already been settled, but in the light of comments made about *Aparajito*, some fundamentals would seem to need restating.

The quantity of matter that a director can put into his film is limited in the first place by considerations of length. This length may vary between an hour and a half, and two and a half hours, limits infused by exigencies of commercial exploitations which hold true of all film-producing countries. While a film of shorter length may have some possibilities of exploration — particularly abroad — a film lasting, say, four hours is a globally untenable proposition. From the very earliest days of feature film-making, stories have been specially written or existing stories and plays adapted to conform to these limits.

Leaving aside original stories, the obvious contention of an existing literary original is that it provides a ready-made theme as story. It may or may not be a popular work, but if it contains material for good cinema, it will attract the perceptive film market. If it lacks filmic possibilities but is a popular work, it will still attract film-makers for its lucrative possibilities; in such a case, the stress will naturally be on the content of the original rather than the form of the adaptation. In a few happy instances, the dimension of the original fits in with the normal film length; the longer short stories of Sarat Chandra and Rabindranath are an example. But in the overwhelming majority of instances, the original will need pruning, condensing and reshaping if it is to achieve integrity as a film. Instances are numerous, but one may mention the films from Dickens (I would urge the critics to compare the book of *Great Expectations* with its masterly film adaptation), Hugo, Jane Austen, Tolstoy, the plays of Shakespeare and Shaw (who himself rewrote *Pygmalion* for the screen), and, of course, works such as Bibhutibhushan Banerjee's *Pather Panchali* and *Aparajito*.

***

It is not difficult to prove that to consider adopting a novel like *Aparajito* in its entirety is out of question. Complaint has been made that I have left out some characters from the novel. "Some" is an understatement. I have left out exactly two hundred and thirty-seven characters. Allotting an average of one minute to each character, we arrive at a running time of a little under four hours. Allowing for an occasional breathing space and the transitional passages, and the time-lapse montages, and the credits …

But let us not go into extremes. *Aparajito* — the film is based on the last third of *Pather Panchali* the novel and the first third of the novel of its name, ending with the death of Sarabjaya and Apu's return to the city to continue his studies. I selected this portion because I felt it contained material for a two-hour long film. I saw its structure and all the exploration establishing the main relationships, a middle passage of development and conflict in terms of character, and a denouncement resolving the major conflicts but avoiding a full close in keeping with the continuity of life which runs through Bibhutibhushan's work.

An important element of this particular portion of this novel is the relationship between mother and son, and I chose this to be the dominant theme of the film. The exposition section — the Benaras episode — does not establish the theme, but creates the condition for it, in the sudden death of the father. This entire section closely follows the book. The deviations that occur in the subsequent portion were made with only one objective in view — to establish and develop the mother-and-son relationship in the simplest and quickest manner possible. Simplicity was essential in the absence of a strong narrative thread — never a feature of Bibhutibhushan's novels (I wonder how many can relate to the story of *Aparajito*!).

The episode in the zamindar's house which follows the death of Harihar is rich enough in incidents to make a full length feature film in detail. But because of the mother's involvement, mentally and physically, in her work and her surroundings, her concern for her son and her possessiveness towards him do not emerge to the extent in this episode that they do in the phase that follows — in the village of Mansapota. The episode in the zamindar's home was therefore taken as a transitional, though obligatory, passage and treated as such.

In the village episode — up to the point of Apu's departure for Calcutta — the deviations are in the nature of dramatic condensation, and there is no departure from the spirit of the original. In the book, Apu finishes his education in a primary school and then decides to continue it in a high school situated in a town far away from the village. This involved a separation from his mother. I decided again — for dramatic reasons — to hold back this separation until the time of Apu's departure for the city to study in college. For this, I had to combine the two schools into one and bring it within walking distance of Apu's village. Another unavoidable omission at this stage was of the charming girl Nirmala, an acquaintance of Apu's high school friend. While I regretted the omission, I had to consider the fact that for a character to be established as being genuinely and positively good and not just outwardly "nice" requires considerable footage. I might even have considered giving this footage if the Nirmala episode had some connection with the main theme. It had none. It was like a short story, admittedly touching, but isolated, and therefore, without claim to a place in a film scenario. I would also like to put on record that the character of Lila, the child as well as the adolescent, was present in the scenario. Its omission from the film version was not dictated by any aesthetic reasons.

***

As shown in the film, Apu's activities in Calcutta are a severe simplification of the original. Deliberately, his struggle is not played up; because to have introduced an element so strong and so rich in development at such a late point in the story would have entirely upset the balance of the film. I felt it was more important to establish the part of Apu's acceptance of acclimatization to city life so that the drama of the following episode could might be played up.

It is the in the sequence of Apu's reaction, with the mother and son together for the last time, that the theme really comes to the fore. The growing tension between the two, the sullen looks, the curt exchanges, the scene of the mother hesitating to wake up the son on the day of his departure — all these will not be found in the book. But they are improvisations on an extraordinarily revealing statement of the author himself. On hearing of his mother's death, says Bibhutibhushan, Apu's first reaction was one of relief, of a freedom from encumbrance. In my opinion, this daring and profound revelation, untranslatable in itself into pure filmic terms, justifies the dramatization of the mother and son relationships. The heartlessness on Apu's part will not seem nearly as shocking when considered in the light of this revelation.

To the eminent critic who wrote that the scene of Apu's weeping at his mother's death was an unwarranted fabrication because the book doesn't mention such an occurrence, I would like to point out that the book also neglects to mention whether Apu spoke with his tongue and ate with his hand and walked on his feet …

"Dangerously near a documentary", warns a critic, which is all the time what we have been aiming at is precisely that feel of the documentary, that outward and inward ring of truth, the hallmark of the best contemporary European cinema, so precious and so hard to achieve. Precious to me as a film-maker, but is it so to our critics? Do they not prefer the old familiar sights and the old familiar sounds — the soothing monotone of the endless dialogue mouthed by the exquisite hero and the more exquisite heroine, within the three walls of the gaudy studio set lit with that charming ambiguity, and the windows looking out on that solid dependable backdrop?

Ray with Apu (Pinaki Sengupta)
during the shooting of *Aparajito*
in Benaras.
Photograph courtesy
Magnum Photos

"Misses the dramatic possibilities of the original" — Pardon me, but the original is not dramatic. Bibhutibhushan is among the least dramatic of the Bengali novelists. What drama there is in *Aparajito* is really at a subtle psychological level. The high-pitched moments in the latter part of the book (such as Lila's suicide) lack the conviction of the other parts.

"Neo realist" — Very well; but look for the source roots not in *Bicycle Thieves* but in Bibhutibhushan himself. Read him carefully and you will find the realism, the humanism, the documentary details and the avoidance of the concocted plot, trumped- up dramatic situations which inform the work of the best neorealists in Europe, and which I tried to preserve in the two films.

"The place (Benaras) has come alive, but not the people". Nonsense. No place comes alive on the screen if its people don't, certainly not Benaras, where even the animals must come alive. The technique adopted from the very first day of the Benaras episode was to combine the life with the locale. There isn't one shot that serves a solely pictorial purpose. If at times the locale has seemed to come too far into the foreground, it is due to an intrinsic quality of the place itself. Those who have been to Benaras know what tremendous visual impact it makes.

FILM-MAKING AS I UNDERSTAND IT

Published in *Cine Advance*, 1958

Since, cinema is a complex art form and it requires knowledge and understanding of several components, techniques to make a good film, how could I, who had never worked in a film and was a commercial artist, achieve such unique perfection with my first film *Pather Panchali*? A relevant question this and this is how I would like to reply.

Although *Pather Panchali* was my first film, I have been passionately wanting to make a film since 1944. I used to make rounds of producers with scenarios for films without any result. As soon as I read a good story, I prepared two treatments for it — one as I would like to make it, and the other as the film would be made by the industry. And strangely my guesses often proved correct. The nearest I got to making a film was Tagore's *Ghare Baire*. I didn't think of *Pather Panchali* till 1947 when I did some illustrations for the children's version of the classic. I prepared the scenario, and sketched the frames. I went to many producers, but finally started the film with my own resources. All the rewards of the world won't make me forget the good art books and records I had to sell. Finances I got later on but …

Of course, influences, direct as well as indirect, have contributed towards the totality of my vision and led me to the two films I have made. I have been deeply impressed by the work of directors like Chaplin, De Sica, Renoir, Clair, Pudovkin and Eisenstien. I think Renoir's *The Southerner* had a great influence on my conception of *Pather Panchali*. I consider De Sica to be the greatest living director — Chaplin, of course, excepted. He is unique. His presence in his own films is such an integral part of the totality of his work that it is wisest to separate him from all others and his *Bicycle Thieves* remains a model for all directors. I have great admiration for certain particular aspect of a director's work … during my short stay in Europe, I was able to see a large number of classical and contemporary work, and this naturally helped me a lot.

As for other influences, I count the two years I spent at Santiniketan under Nandalal Bose to be the most fruitful of my formative years. His way of looking at nature, his profound humanisms, the documentary humanism in Cartier-Bresson's photography also taught me to look at people and places selectively. It was at Santiniketan that I came across Paul Rotha's film book and that aroused my interest in serious cinema. Then I read up all the books I could get hold of on the subject.

Which means I saw the films much later. I actually became seriously interested in the cinema through books. And the same thing happened with Western classical music also. I was drawn to it after I read the biography of Beethoven by Thayer some twenty years back. Neorealism is often talked of in connection with my work. But I don't think there is any such thing as the neorealist style. Neo-realist is an attitude and not a style. The story may lack a conventional plot, it will just offer a slice of life, it will say "this is real, this could happen" … It may lack strong contrasts, yet help to discover something unobserved. A film like *Bicycle Thieves* or even more appropriately *Umberto D*. I think the style of a particular film is dictated by its theme. Actually, it is this stylistic consistency in a film that makes it a work of art.

Directors like Hitchcock, Kazan, Cocteau, Orsen Welles have a strong stamp of their individuality on their films due to their preferences for a particular subject. You will notice there are certain mannerisms, certain cinematic phrases which a director might prefer. Take, for instance, Hitchcock. He doesn't make anything but suspense films. Or the violence and sex in Kazan.

But one of my current films *Jalsaghar* has quite a different feel as compared to the other three — *Pather Panchali*, *Aparajito* and *Parash Pathar*. Here, music plays an extremely important part, not merely to heighten drama but one must say as a dramatic element; the film also requires sophisticated acting and I am using almost exclusively professional actors. Here I look at the disintegration of feudalism from the top of the pyramid. I wanted to make a comedy picture which I am making now in *Parash Pathar*. I feel there should be great possibilities for developing a comedy tradition in Bengali films.

The way I feel now, I want to concentrate on contemporary themes or at least stories within living memory. I like to relate my work to living realities. And in case it is not possible to make good period or historical films in the context of the existing Bengali film industry.

At present, I have no desire to make Hindi films. I feel art must be rooted in life. I have to make films within my own national cultural complex, the language and region I know, the nuances I feel. I think Hindi films made in Bombay particularly fail due to absence of the link, due to the polyglot and amorphous character of the false culture that prevails in the industry there. You will find Bengali and Marathi films on an average are far better than Bombay productions due to this. And in any case, a truly national film is never lacking in universal appeal. I believe that both in *Aparajito* and *Pather Panchali*, I have been able to communicate some essentially Bengali experiences in universally comprehensible terms.

Now, about these two films, *Pather Panchali* and *Aparajito*. They are, in fact, two completely different films. It was possible in *Pather Panchali* to establish an integration between nature and life that one is able to achieve in rare instances. This of course was inherent in Bibhutibushan Bandyopadhyay's great classic. There was complete unity in the theme in spite of the tremendous range of characters. Yet, there are things in *Pather Panchali* which I consider clumsy and in certain ways immature. In this respect, *Aparajito* is a more mature and satisfying film. It was a difficult film to make and I suppose, in a way, a difficult film to appreciate. I have told the story of this cathartic tragedy with the utmost economy of visual and aural phrases. It is always difficult to appreciate changing backgrounds in one film. I think it is a film which, perhaps, should be seen twice. Also the inner world of mother and son is intensely introspective and middle-class factors restricted the appeal; but I have found many non-Bengalis, both foreigners and Indians, quite receptive to the sensitivity of the treatment. In the ultimate analysis, the film, like other media of creative expression, has to be judged on its intentions. The trouble in

India is that even amongst the intelligentsia the film language is practically unknown and I suppose it will take many directors and quite a long time to generate some intelligent appreciation of the the medium.

It certainly requires research and analysis to find out why songs should be so inevitable in what supposedly are dramatic films. But I think it is easy to explain why it is kept in continuance. This is a trend which has been nurtured and tested at the box office. It has nothing to do with filmic property. If you can sell your songs you have sold the film. Just as you sell the stars, sometimes a chimpanzee.

STATEMENT ON THE APU TRILOGY

Sourced from Ray's notebook, previously unpublished

The three films of the Apu Trilogy — *Pather Panchali*, *Aparajito* and *The World of Apu* — were based on two novels by one of the finest novelists of Bengal — Bibhutibhushan Bandyopadhyay. The first novel — *Pather Panchali*, won immediate acclaim on publication for its lyricism, humanism and its remarkably aesthetic depiction of life in rural Bengal in the third decade of the present century.

As one born and bred on the city, I had no contact with the village; but the novel was something like an encyclopedia of rural life. This was proved beyond doubt when we actually started shooting the first film on rural location.

While I learnt a lot about the art of film-making from watching Hollywood films of the forties and fifties, my primary influences when I started my first film were Jean Renoir and the DeSica of *Bicycle Thieves* and *Umberto D*. And yet, soon after I started shooting, I realized that the form, rhythm and texture of my film would derive from elements which were deeply rooted in my own culture, which had little to do with the culture of France and Italy.

When I was at work on *Pather Panchali*, I had no thought of making a Trilogy. After the world-wide success of the film, I decided to continue with the same story — still not thinking in terms of a Trilogy. It was in Venice in 1957, at the Press Conference after the screening of *Aparajito*, that I was asked if I had a Trilogy in mind. I found myself saying "Yes" — somewhat rashly, because I still didn't know whether the second part contained

Statement on the Apu Trilogy

The three films of the Apu Trilogy — Pather Panchali, Aparajito & The World of Apu — were based on two novels by one of the finest novelists of Bengal — Bibhutibhusan Banerji. The first novel — Pather Panchali, won immediate acclaim on publication for its lyricism, humanism & its remarkably authentic depiction of life in rural Bengal in the 3rd decade of the present century.

As one born and bred in the city, I had no contact with the village; but the novel was something like an encyclopaedia of rural life. This was proved beyond doubt when we actually started shooting the first film on rural locations.

While I learnt a lot about the craft of film making

2

from watching Hollywood films of the 40's & 50's,
my primary influences when I started my first
film were Jean Renoir & the De Sica of Bicycle
Thief & Umberto D. But yet, soon after
I started shooting, I realised that the form,
                                                        derive
rhythm & texture of my film would ~~derive~~ ~
from elements which were deeply rooted in
my own culture, which had little to do with
the culture of France or Italy.

        When I was at work on Pather Panchali,
I had no thought of making a Trilogy). After the
world-wide success of the film, I decided to
continue with the Apu story — still not thinking
in terms of a Trilogy. It was in Venice in 1957,
~~after the~~ at the Press Conference after the
                          that
screening of Aparajito, I was asked if I had a
Trilogy in mind. I found myself saying "yes".—

Facsimile of the Statement on the *Apu Trilogy* (Second page)

3

somewhat rashly, because I still didn't know whether
the second novel contained the material for a
third film. As it turned out, it did,
and the Trilogy was completed with The World
of Apu.

It was the Trilogy that shaped my style
and sharpened my craft as a film maker,
and my debt to the author of the two novels—
rather than to any films or film makers of
the West — is immeasurable.

Facsimile of the Statement on the *Apu Trilogy* (Third page)

Ray with Subrata Mitra during the shooting of *Aparajito*. Photograph courtesy Magnum Photos

the material for a third film. As it turned out, it did, and the Trilogy was completed with *The World of Apu*.

It was the Trilogy that shaped my style and sharpened my craft as a film-maker, and my debt to the author of the two novels — rather than to any film and film-maker of the West — is immeasurable.

"EXQUISITE...PROFOUND... MAGICAL...HUMOROUS!"

Another exquisite motion picture embracing the timeless flow of life in India has rolled from the eloquent camera of the protean Satyajit Ray. It penetrates the surface of Indian culture to touch the universal heart of men...a rare experience.

A BLEND OF POETIC CREATION THAT IS ALMOST MAJESTIC!"
—Bosley Crowther, New York Times

"A Complete Creation

—dealing with the hungers, pains and joys of youth in terms of compassionate understanding and truth, underlined by haunting tenderness, subtle sophistication and mature wisdom!"
—Judith Crist, Herald Tribune

"WONDERFUL ARTISTRY... CLEAR AND EXTRAORDINARILY GRAPHIC!"
— Archer Winsten, New York Post

"WORK OF GENIUS!"
—Justin Gilbert, Daily Mirror

"EACH STORY IS A GEM!"
—Alton Cook, World Telegram-Sun

"A TWIN TRIUMPH!"
—Newsweek

SATYAJIT RAY'S

Two Daughters

A Janus Films release

Press-folder of *Two Daughters* used for USA release (1961)

TWO DAUGHTERS

Article sourced from Ray's notebook (c. 1961), previously unpublished

I have often regretted the fact that there were so few short story films. Surely, one would have thought, they have as much right to exist as an art form as their literary equivalent. In India — and more particularly in Bengal, which is my home — the short story is a flourishing literary form. The poet Tagore himself wrote well over a hundred — an output of amazing diversity which pretty well exhausts the whole gamut of human feelings. There is, in fact, less dispute over the greatness of his short stories than of his poems, and the frequent comparison with Chekov is by no means an idle one. Both *Postmaster* and *Samapti* which comprise *Two Daughters*, as well as a good many others he wrote, bring the Russian master to mind.

I knew I would have to turn to Tagore sooner or later for film subjects. The centenary of the poet's birth in 1961 provided an excellent excuse. *Two Daughters* was really as much a homage to Tagore as a fulfilment of a long felt urge to make short story films.

The choice of these particular stories as against at least fifty other equally translatable ones was naturally dictated by my own temperament. In re-reading the stories, my sympathies turned the quickest to Ratan, the wistful little waif of *Postmaster*, grown beyond her years, holding her grief with a stubbornness befitting an adult four times her age — and to Mrinmoyee, the rustic tomboy of *Samapti* whose marriage with a young scholar from the city gives rise to such hectic developments. Both these films provided opportunities for exploring the subtle nuances of human relationships that have fascinated

শততম রবীন্দ্র-জয়ন্তী উপলক্ষে
সত্যজিৎ রায় প্রোডাকসন্স-এর
অভিনব চিত্রাঞ্জলি

একসঙ্গে
রবীন্দ্রনাথের
তিনটি গল্পের
চিত্ররূপ

তীন
কন্যা

প্রযোজনা
চিত্রনাট্য, সংগীত
ও পরিচালনা   সত্যজিৎ রায়

পরিবেশক ছায়াবাণী প্রাইভেট লিমিটেড

চলচ্চিত্রের ইতিহাসে প্রথম
বহির্বিশ্ব ও সর্বভারতীয় শুভমুক্তি
৫ই মে!
ন্যাশনাল থিয়েটার (লন্ডন) ● এক্সেলসিয়ার থিয়েটার
(বম্বে) ● রিগ্যাল (নিউ দিল্লি) ● মিনার্ভা টকিজ
(মাদ্রাজ) ● চৌধুরী টকিজ (গৌহাটি, আসাম)

রূপবাণী   ০   ভারতী   ০   অরুণা
ও শহরতলীর সর্বত্র!

Newspaper advertisement in Bengali designed by Ray
for worldwide release of *Teen Kanya* in 1961

me ever since my first film, *Pather Panchali*.

The main problem in *Samapti*, from the cinematic point of view, was to convey the fact of Mrinmoyee suddenly, almost magically, outgrowing her adolescence. Tagore conveys this in a single line of lyrical prose. One could do it with words in the film too, of course. "Mother, I think there's something happening inside of me. I don't want to go out and play with the boys anymore," or words to that effect. But such devices didn't appeal to me; I strongly believe that the most crucial developments in a film should be conveyed as far as possible in predominantly visual terms. I write my own dialogue, and like doing it, but I still find grappling with visual problems a far more exciting task than finding the right words to put into the mouths of my characters. Thus it was that the squirrel motif in *Samapti* came into being.

Mrinmoyee and Ratan are both played in the film by newcomers. I discovered (I generally do my own talent scouting) — Chandana Bannerji in a dancing school taking her first lessons in Bharatanatyam. A pair of myopic glasses couldn't hide the glint in her eyes, and the buck tooth showed with the very first words she spoke. Aparna Das Gupta, who plays Mrinmoyee, was the daughter of a film critic friend of mine, and was doing her last term at school. The rest of the cast was mainly professional. As always, I found it helped to have the pros and the non-pros playing together. The non-pros feel flattered and elated to be put on a par with the pros, while the pros, faced with the competition of untutored ease and unnaturalness, find themselves suppressing their mannerisms.

Postmaster was shot in one week in a village only five miles beyond the city limits to the south of Calcutta. When the wind blew in from the north, it brought with it the faint buzz of city traffic. And yet, there were snakes and lizards around, and insects we barely knew the names of.

For *Samapti,* we had to move a hundred and fifty miles to the east. The river in the film, the famous Padma, runs between Bengal and Pakistan, and if you rowed out beyond a certain point, you would be trespassing on foreign waters. We chose the rainy season because we needed muddy roads for a certain key scene. The river was in full flow fringed with muddy water. The Padma flowed. But we found the roads to be dry. It hadn't, we were told, rained hard enough. We prayed for rain, but it didn't come. On the last day of our shoot, we took buckets and hosepipes and garden sprays and set about watering the road with pondwater. We did this for four hours, and then we watched the parched earth soak up each bucketful in a monstrous, unquenchable thirst. And then the shower came, the best awesome downpour you can think of, and in less than ten minutes we had all the mud and slush and puddles we needed. And we had our shots.

LETTER TO THE ILLUSTRATED WEEKLY OF INDIA

Published in *The Illustrated Weekly of India,* 28 February, 1965

I wish to make some comments on Chidananda Das Gupta's article entitled "Towards Better Film Music". I am gratified that Das Gupta likes my music for *Charulata* and the ESSO "Short", but about the former, he makes some erroneous statements which I must hasten to correct. It is true that the title music of *Charulata* uses the melody of a Tagore song, and that variations of parts of this melody constitute some further material for the background music; but to say that the background music is composed "purely in terms of variations on a theme from Tagore" is wrong.

There are actually four main musical motifs in the film, two of which are original compositions. The first, which is the first piece of music to occur in the main body of the film, is used as an evocation of Charulata's loneliness. This is the principal musical motifs, and occurs six times in the film. The second original motif is first heard with the first hint of the tragic outcome of the story: in the scene where Charu breaks down in the presence of Amal and reveals the true, nature of her feelings. This motif, written for the lower strings, really comes into its own in the scene in the printing press where Amal discovers Bhupati in a state of profound disillusionment. A third motif is based on the Scotch tune that also serves as the basis for the Tagore song "Phooley Phooley" which both Amal and Charu sing in the film. The longest single piece of music in the film — in the scene where Bhupati and Amal expatiate on the charms of England — is based on this tune. The fourth motif is, of course, based on the Tagore song that Das Gupta mentions. But this occurs invariably

A still from *Charulata*

in combination with one or more of the three other motifs mentioned.

Besides these four, and their variations, the film uses other music in snatches as well as in extended compositions which have nothing to do with Tagore. The second longest piece of music in the film accompanies Charu's recollection of her childhood. This has a Bengali folk basis. In terms of duration, the Tagore music takes up eleven minutes out of a total of nearly forty-five minutes of background music.

I do not agree with Das Gupta's contention that Tagore songs provide a more exploitable source of background music. On the contrary, because these songs have a too clearly marked formal pattern, I feel they can be used only at the risk of drawing attention away from the film.

It is also surely an exaggeration to say that "Tagore's melodies inevitably parallel his description in words, be it of a mood or a landscape, a time of day or a season". For songs that relate to a particular season or time of day, Tagore invariably used classical ragas which have an age-old association with such seasons and times of day. Landscapes,

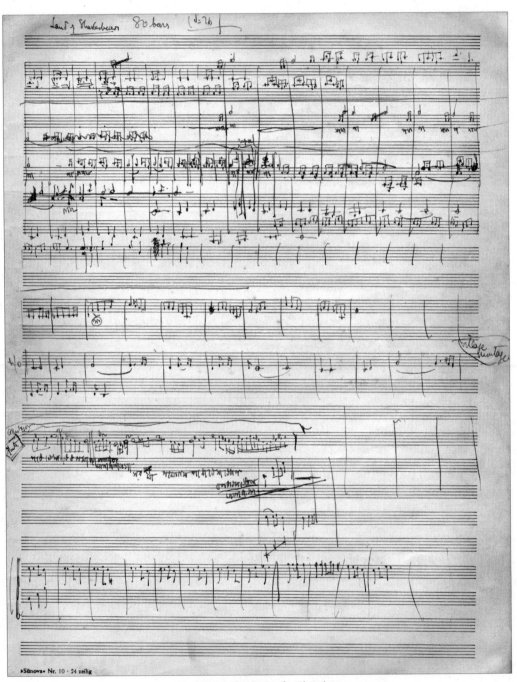

Musical notation by Ray for *Charulata*

so far as my knowledge of music goes, have never been suggested with any precision by any music, except, and even then only vaguely, by some blatantly naturalistic programme music of the West. As for moods, Tagore did often achieve a remarkable correspondence between words and tunes, but never to the highly improbable extent of suggesting any but the most basic emotional states. Such music, by itself, is really quite incapable of reflecting the complex moods that invest a modern psychological film. One is, therefore, obliged to compose original music. And whether such music has roots in the East or the West, or is derived from a Tagore song or a classical raga or a folk tune, is quite immaterial.

Das Gupta characterizes Vanraj Bhatia's music for Shanti Choudhury's documentary as "orchestration of Indian music". This is not correct. In this principal theme, Bhatia uses string writing of a totally Western, contrapuntal, Beethoven-late-quartetish idiom, and juxtaposes it, very effectively, with a simply orchestrated, folk-based Indian melody. To compare this, as Das Gupta does, with the work of composers like Ali Akbar Khan and Ravi Shankar, who are untrained in contrapunctal writing, is wrong. Das Gupta also implies that composers like Ali Akbar Khan and Ravi Shankar work better under "a sensitive director like Satyajit Ray, Ritwick Ghatak and Mrinal Sen". Of the two composers, only the former has worked with Ghatak, and that too only once. Neither has ever worked with Mrinal Sen, who uses commercial composers with less perspicacity than most other directors of repute. To say Ali Akbar Khan and Ravi Shankar have worked well only under sensitive directors is to imply that it is possible for an insensitive film to have a sensitive musical score. Surely, Das Gupta should realize that no musical score, however good in itself, is ever known to have served any aesthetic purpose in an indifferent film, and is unlikely to provide any inspiration to a composer, which makes it incumbent on a critic to judge a composer only on the basis of his work for films which are good in themselves.

THE SILENT ERA

This article was written on the occasion of a film session of selected silent films;
Published in *Chitravas*, Vol.1, No.1, 1966

A man called Edwin Porter discovered one fine morning that you could tell stories with moving pictures just as you could tell them with words: and he proceeded on this assumption to make a film called *The Great Train Robbery*. The year was 1906, the place was America.

Did Porter know that in making the film he was laying the foundation for the most powerful art form of the twentieth century — the only art form whose birth and evolution are part of recorded history? I doubt it. However, let us take a quick look at what was happening in the world of arts in Europe around the time of *The Great Indian Robbery*.

In 1906, in the world of painting, Picasso was nearing the end of his blue period but there were still two years to go before the first Cubist landscape would emerge, Cezanne had just died, but Renoir was still active and approaching the height of his powers.

In music, Stravinsky was about to join forces with Diaghileff to write the scores for some of the most original and striking productions of modern ballet. Elsewhere, the seeds of modern music had already been laid by composers like Schonberg and Bartok.

In the theatre, Shaw in England was writing *Major Barbara*; Gordon Graig had just published his *Art of the Theatre*; and Stanislavsky in Russia was engaged in meticulous and revolutionary productions of the latest plays of Anton Chekov.

One would have thought that in Europe, where so many intellectuals were engaged in such diverse artistic pursuits, the potentialities of a new art form would be recognized and seized at in no time. But such was not to be. Europe at this point was really too content with its traditional forms to take more than a cursory interest in the new medium, although one must mention the Frenchman who did have some fun with the movie camera and produced what is now generally regarded as the first genuine primitive films.

The cinema, in fact, was obliged to discover its roots in a country which had no traditions of its own at all, the United States of America. If it was Edwin Porter who found that you could tell stories with a camera, it was left to a far more talented man —another American — to raise the film to the level of art.

As one who has come into the field at an advanced stage in the development of the medium, I can't help marvelling at the way the pioneers made discoveries about unique properties of the brand new art form. What an extraordinary thrill it must have been to Griffith to realize that you could move your camera close to an actor, catch a movement of his eyes and convey a shade or feeling that no actor on the stage could ever hope to convey to his audience. Or that you could put your camera on a hilltop and convey the movement of a whole army, to fill the theatre with the surge and excitement of a real battle. Equally exciting must have been the discovery that you could actually join separate shots so that they made sense, just as a string of words forming a sentence made sense.

Then again, in films you arranged forms in a rectangular space as you did in painting. But, and this is the exciting revelation, if your objects moved or your camera moved, or both moved at the same time, a new set of laws suddenly began to operate and you found yourself thinking of dancing or the art of ballet.

Then there was the affinity with music. It is a significant fact that all the pioneers of the cinema are known to have loved and known a great deal about music. Griffith used to speak of the inspiration that he derived from the music of Beethoven, and one can actually spot the symphonic structure underlying films like *The Birth of a Nation* and *Intolerance*.

This is hardly surprising. Film is the only art, apart from music, which exists in time. We respond to music because our nerves are made to respond to certain qualities inherent in music — qualities of rhythm, of movement, of contrast. A good film has to have these qualities too. Without them the best of stories would be told badly and, therefore, ineffectually. In a film, those qualities cannot be reduced to mathematical terms, as they

1. CHAPLIN - GOLD RUSH
2. KEATON - The General
3. DREYER - The Passion of Joan of Arc
4. NIKOLAI EKK - Road to Life.
5. EISENSTEIN - Ivan the Terrible I + II
6. DOVZHENKO - Earth
7. JOHN FORD - My Darling Clementine
8. FRANK CAPRA - Mr Smith Goes to Washington
9. WILLIAM WYLER - Little Foxes
10. BILLY WILDER - Double Indemnity
11. DAVID LEAN - Brief Encounter / Great Expectations
12. CAROL REED - Fallen Idol
13. JOHN HUSTON - Maltese Falcon
14. ORSON WELLES - Citizen Kane
15. LEWIS MILESTONE - A Walk in the Sun
16. MARK SANDRICH - Top Hat
17. SAM WOOD - A Night at the Opera
18. JEAN RENOIR - La Règle du Jeu
19. INGMAR BERGMAN - Cries & Whispers
20. VITTORIO DE SICA - Bicycle Thieves
21. MICHELANGELO ANTONIONI - La Notte
22. AKIRA KUROSAWA - Seven Samurai
23. KENZI MIZOGUCHI - Ugetsu Monogatari
24. YASUJIRO OZU - Tokyo Story
25. FRANCOIS TRUFFAUT - 400 Blows
26. MURNAU - Nosferatu
27. WIENE - Dr Caligari

28 SYDNEY LUMET - 12 Angry Men
29 LUBITSCH - Trouble in Paradise
30 HITCHCOCK - REAR WINDOW
31 MAMOULIAN - Dr Jekyll & Mr Hyde
32 MILOS FORMAN - Taking Off
33 ALAN J PAKULA - Klute
34 DUVIVIER - Un Carnet de Bal
35 POLANSKI - Chinatown
36 WOODY ALLEN - Interiors
37 CARLOS SAURA - Cousin Angelica
38 FLAHERTY - Man of Aran
39 GEORGE ROY HILL - Butch Cassidy & the Sundance Kid
40 MAX OPHÜLS - Letter from an Unknown Woman
41 KOZINTSEV - King Lear
42 RENQUIER - Farrebique
43 FELLINI - 8½

Ray's list of his favourite films in his notebook contains many silent era gems

can be in music. They remain indefinable and elusive — but they can be felt. And it is these qualities, and not turns and twists of plot, that make you want to see a great film again and again.

It is astonishing that there should still be people who doubt the claims of the cinema to be regarded as art. They say films do not have the purity of painting or the abstract qualities of music or the analytical scope of a novel or the dramatic intensity of the theatre. To me, this tendency to run down an art form because it does not have certain properties of some other art forms, or to look for traits which by its very nature the art form cannot possess, seems childish and pointless.

Perhaps the trouble started with the coming of sound when the cinema began to derive more and more from the theatre and the written word. The trash that has been perpetrated in the era of sound in the name of art or box office or God knows what is beyond measure. It is ironical that this deviation from the path of art, should have taken place first in the land which indicated the true status of the cinema. At any rate, it has taken all of thirty years for the cinema to find its bearings again and for true artists to begin emerging from the rubble and a new set of aesthetics to be formulated.

At long last, we know the cinema for what it is, a language, an enormously flexible and potent language, a language that can be used in just as many different ways as you can use the language of words. In the silent era, it was a language of images. Ever since the talkies ruthlessly replaced the silent film, it has been a language of image and sound.

I say ruthlessly because I believe the silent film to be an entirely different form of art from the sound film, and there is no aesthetic justification for one replacing the other. Chaplin did not regret the coming of sound film as much as he regretted the inevitable consequences: the strangulation of an already speechless art. To the lay public, whose only interest lay in novelty, it appeared that sound was liberating the cinema from some constricting limitation — almost as if the film without the tongue was an unfortunate cripple, and the chap with the microphone had come to perform a miracle of surgery.

Of course, it was nothing of the kind. What sound actually did was to bring the cinema to reality. But in doing so, it inadvertently unleashed all manner of forces which tended to pull the cinema away from its goal of art. Films were now more life-like —

everybody said. There were men and women who talked and talked like you and me and did not do odd things with their limbs and their eyeballs. If the silent cinema was art, who cares? This was life — or as near life as you could hope to get without actually getting involved in it. And you only had to pay a little cash at the box office, lean back in your plush seat and glance up at the charmed rectangle. This was cinema — this was what we had all been waiting for!

No wonder the silent films made a silent exit.

All this is not meant to belittle the sound cinema. I could not do it, being so happily involved in it myself. The point I am trying to make is that the sound film is not an improvement on the silent film but a completely separate art form with its own special appeal and its own special aesthetics. Really, the two should have existed side by side. The fact that they could not only goes to show the cruel illogicality of commercial pressures that decide the fate of films and film-makers.

It is because the silent cinema has been dead for so long and we see so little of it that we see it as something remote and archaic. We respect it, but cannot quite warm up to it. I hope the present session will instil in us the love that it deserves.

It is a pity that the series contains nothing by Griffith or Strohein and more of the early slapstick comedies. But what there is, is nevertheless considerable. We are going to see what some of the great European film-makers did with the medium after they had absorbed the lesson of the American pioneers. Not at all the films have equal or consistent aesthetic value. We must remember that the medium was comparatively unfamiliar and was still being explored. But I think the very fact of the exploration and the way it is revealed in the films should be of very great interest to true lovers of the cinema.

The Cabinet of Dr. Caligari, for instance, is an exploration in the sense that it attempts to do in films what the Expressionists in Germany were doing on the stage and in painting. This particular experiment has never been repeated and *Caligari* remains something of a freak — although a fascinating one. *Caligari* was, in fact, an aesthetic mistake because it ignored the special genius of the movie camera and attempted to impose on the cinema the qualities of an alien art.

René Clair's two films — *Le Million* and *The Italian Straw Hat* — derive clearly from Chaplin. But they have enough of the essential French quality to prove that Clair had completely absorbed the lesson of his master and had, in fact, evolved a style that was peculiarly his own.

The Last Laugh I find interesting for several reasons. There is, for instance, the fluency of its camera and the fact that the director was able to tell the story without the aid of a single title. The other reason is a more complex one. *The Last Laugh* was made at a time when the Germans had already acquired enormous technical efficiency. One of the effects of this, and this was to spread to Hollywood, was an over-confidence in their designers and their cameramen. An entire hotel with a busy street outside was built and photographed in the studio for the film. Now, this dependence on the expert simulators of nature can be a dangerous thing. It tends to confine you within the four walls of a studio to the extent that you finally forget how the light of nature plays on the surface of things and what moods it creates and how well the movie camera can capture such moods. All the early masters had a true respect for natural light. Stroheim once went to shoot some scenes for his film *Greed*, in an apartment house in San Francisco. He was after "truth", he said. But the light inside the room was not strong enough. His production manager was worried. "Don't you think, Mr. Stroheim, that it would be better to build some rooms in the studio?" he asked. "No!" said Stroheim. "We place the camera here and shoot. And for light we pull down the wall behind us," — and he did just that!

So much has been written about *Battleship Potemkin* that I don't wish to add anything to it. *Potemkin* was one of the two in the present series which was included among the six greatest films of all time. The selection was made at Brussels in 1958 by a jury of which I happened to be one of the members. There were a total of twenty films which had already been selected by film historians and critics, and we directors were asked to name the six that we considered were still of value to the modern film-maker. The seven of us sat arguing for eleven hours before we came to a decision. But there was no argument about Potemkin; nor about the other film — which was Carl Dreyer's *The Passion of Joan of Arc*.

For me, *The Passion of Joan of Arc* represents the summit of the silent cinema if you leave out the comedies of Chaplin and Buster Keaton. It is the one film in the present series that has not dated one bit in its psychological exploration and the means employed

Poster of *The Passion of Joan of Arc*

for this purpose and it is as modern as Antonioni. It contains the best single performance ever recorded in a film — a performance that has got nothing of the theatre in it. In the precision and expressive range of its photography, in the depths of its emotional intensity and the simplicity and exactitude of the means employed, it remains the greatest single reason for the cinema to be regarded as art and for the silent cinema to be considered as a valid and self-sufficient form of expression.

WHY NOT HINDI?

Published in *Filmfare*, 24 June 1966

A question I have often been asked by journalists as well as well-meaning non-Bengali friends is: Why don't you make Hindi films? To this I have always given the obvious and cogent answer: I don't, because I don't know Hindi well enough. "Well, why don't you learn it?" Of course I could learn it; and in all likelihood it wouldn't take me very long, because I already have a smattering of it. Well, then, why don't I go ahead and do it?

Before I answer that, I would like to point out that the question would probably not have come up at all if the practice of Bengali directors migrating to Bombay and settling there to make Hindi films hadn't existed for such a long time. An English director would think it very odd to be asked why he didn't go to France to make French films, although he were an educated person, he would more likely to be fluent in French than an educated Bengali would be in Hindi.

With the exception of Bimal Roy, whose *Do Bigha Zamin* remains his finest achievement, and, to some extent, Nitin Bose, Bengali directors who went to work in Bombay revealed too quickly and too clearly the real reasons for migration — which were economic and not artistic.

It is true that there is more money in Bombay, and it is also true that I am not proof against the allurement of big money; but if big money means forfeiting even a fraction of

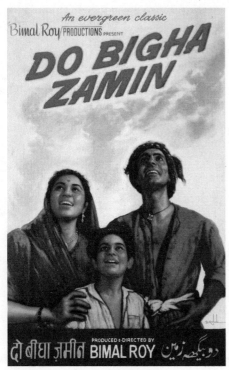

Poster of *Do Bigha Zamin*

the "kick" that I get out of film-making in all its stages of writing, directing and cutting, then I'd sooner give it a wide berth.

Even if I were to learn Hindi, I know I could learn only enough to speak it, and to understand (broadly, not in its nuances) the dialogue that someone else would write for my film. I would never know whether the writer has provided me with true filmic dialogue, or with the sort that even highly paid professionals usually turn out — overwritten, essentially literary stuff which reduces everything to words without taking into account the power of the expressive gesture on the screen. I would, also, never be sure whether a certain expression used by the writer for a character belonging to a particular social status, and speaking in a particular emotional state, was in fact the best one to use in that context. Nor would I know if the dialogue had the all-important quality of verisimilitude, which is more a matter of feeling and observation and retentive memory, than of literary ability. Expressive filmic dialogue is a powerful weapon in the hands of the director, because not only characterization, but the clear and forceful exposition of the theme itself depends on it. I don't think I would ever feel confident if I were to entrust this vital aspect to someone else and not be in a position to judge his work.

Acting, too, is largely guided and shaped by the dialogue. Good dialogue provides an automatic check on an actor's theatrical impulses. It is only when he feels the easy rhythm of lifelike speech that he is able to act without affection. A good actor instinctively feels if his lines are "right" or "wrong"; and the best actor in the world is helpless in the face of high-flown words and long unbroken sentences which turn him into a mouthpiece instead of a human being. Knowledge of literary Hindi is barely enough to prevent such disasters from happening.

There is a long-standing practice of making Hindi films from Bengali stories. The usual procedure with the classics has been merely to translate the dialogue and keep the setting intact. This may work for a non-Bengali audience, but it would certainly not work for me, as I would be acutely conscious of the incongruity of the whole thing. No sensitive Bengali director can get any artistic pleasure out of such a chore, because he would be aware that there is no justification for such a venture beyond the purely commercial one of reaching a wider market.

There are some Bengali stories that lend themselves to adaptation, but they are not as plentiful as one might imagine, because a good story is usually firmly rooted in a particular place, although it may possess certain elements of universality. Hindi films, like *Do Bigha Zamin*, should have a valid artistic reason for being in Hindi. They should exist in their own right, and exude their own unique flavour. Ideally, they should be made by directors who have lived and breathed in that atmosphere, and know the language in all its nuances. I just happen to be not one of them.

WHY DO I MAKE FILMS?

The text of the commentary, written and spoken by Satyajit Ray for B.D.Garga's two-reeler film "Creative Artists of India: Satyajit Ray". Published in *Montage Special Issue* on Ray, July 1966

If someone were to ask me why I make films, I wouldn't find it easy to answer. Not because they aren't any good and right reasons for my making them, but because there are so many.

I think the truest answer would be that I make films for the love of it.

I enjoy every moment of the filmmaking process. I write my own scenario and my own dialogue. And, I find it fascinating to do so.

I select my own actors — sometimes from among the professionals, sometimes right from the street, and when I do that, it seems to me that casting is great fun, because you're actually looking for flesh-and-blood incarnations of the characters you've dreamt up in the process of writing.

Sometimes, you have to work hard with your actors. Sometimes, even an amateur, in his very first appearance before the camera, will do just the thing you want him to do in the very first take.

Shooting, of course, is the great occasion for the marshalling of forces. You as the director, must plan and execute the strategy, whereby man and machine will work in harmony to complement each other. This is hard work and needs any amount of patience. But the exhilaration of a shot well-planned and well-taken makes it all seem worthwhile.

Editing is exciting too, but the excitement is on an intellectual level, and it is controlled and subdued by the need for precision and tenderness in the handling of what — by the mere process of joining — begins to show signs of an independent life.

Apart from the actual creative work, film-making is exciting because it brings me closer to my country and my people. Each film contributes to a process of self-education, making me conscious of the enormous diversity of life around me. I find myself trying, through my films, to trace the underlying pattern that binds this life together. It is the true stuff of the cinema — this dizzying contrast of sight and sound and milieu. And, it's a challenge for any filmmaker to try and orchestrate it and shape its various conflicting elements into a work of art.

Before I made my first film — *Pather Panchali* — I had only a superficial knowledge of what life in a Bengali village was like. Now, I know a good deal about it. I know its soil; its seasons, its trees and forests and flowers; I know how man in the field works and how the women at the well gossip; and I know the children out in the sun and the rain, behaving as well children in all parts of the world do.

My own city of Calcutta, too, I know much better now that I've made a film about it. It isn't quite like any other city in the world to look at. Yet, people are born here and live and make love and earn bread as they do in London and New York and Tokyo.

And, this is what amazes you most and makes you feel indebted to the cinema: this discovery that although you have roots here — in Bengal, in India — you are at the same time part of a large plan, a universal pattern. This uniqueness and thus universality and the co-existence of the two, is what I mainly try to convey through my films.

A LOOK AT THE
SCIENCE FICTION FILMS

Published in *Amrita Bazar Patrika* Puja Annual, 1966

Science fiction and espionage stories are said to be gradually displacing the thriller and the whodunit from their position of eminence in the field of light reading. I don't know what has caused the Spy Boom — probably James Bond — but science fiction was bound to come into its own in an era of rapid technological advance, when even the layman's imagination is being tickled by close-up photos of the surface of the moon, and of astronauts floating weightlessly in space.

In itself, science fiction is not a new thing. In the form in which we know it today, it has existed for at least a century, ever since Jules Verne wrote *Five Weeks in a Balloon*. Verne remained a lone practitioner until H.G. Wells came out with *The Time Machine* and followed it up with a dozen or so of his celebrated imaginary adventures.

By the end of the first decade of the present century, the new genres may be said to have taken roots, and ever since then, they have continued to be enriched sporadically. The present state of luxurious growth is a post-World War II phenomenon, with the USA, Britain, France, Soviet Russia and Czechoslovakia, all contributing to the mainstream.

The cinema has reflected a similar growth in science fiction ever since George Melies of France made *A Trip to the Moon* and other similar fantasies way back in the primitive days of the silent cinema. Melies was primarily out to entertain his simple audience with "special effects". This is not surprising, since the illusionist possibilities of the motion picture were bound to strike the more inventive and frolicsome of the pioneers. And we should remember that Melies was a fellow countryman of Verne.

But Melies's scale was small, as it had to be in those days. The big fantasies had to wait until the 1920s when Germany came out triumphantly with Fritz Lang's ambitious *Metropolis*. This was a futuristic fantasy which triumphed by virtue of its designing and execution: no one excelled the Germans in craftsmanship in those days. The subject of the film was the human situation in a world dominated by machines. This had been a favourite theme of the science-fiction writers, and H.G. Wells himself was to write a similar prophetic story called *The Shape of Things to Come*. This was filmed by Alexander Jordan and was the biggest film to have come out of a British Studio in the thirties.

Both *Metropolis* and *The Shape of Things to Come* set out to shun the imagination with spectacle. Of course, they had their social messages too. But since they looked several centuries ahead, the contemporary viewer felt little emotional involvement with the issues. In other worlds, they were cold looks into the future.

This particular preoccupation is not very much in vogue these days — at least not in films. Now there are new themes and new categories — so many of them, in fact, that it is no longer possible to lump together all science-fiction films, as it was even twenty years ago.

For instance, there is one category — rather low in the scale — which deals with "monsters" which are usually known or unknown species of prehistoric animals which may emerge from the depths of the ocean, or be freed by some explosion — atomic or otherwise — from a state of refrigeration somewhere in the polar regions.

Another category, slightly higher up, takes ordinary, harmless, creatures like ants or flies or spiders, and has them undergo mutant to monstrous proportions through some accident of science or nature.

A third category pits man against the forces of alien planets. This one has subdivisions, because you can have man going out to other planets or you can have aliens descending on Earth. You can even have aliens exerting influence by remote control, so that man is faced with the menace in a disembodied form, so to say.

The fourth and the last category finds man menaced by his own technology. This is, of course, the classical Frankenstein situation, but the variations it has brought forth are numerous. The Robot, which takes the place of the monster in the Frankenstein story, has been featured both wittily and terrifyingly in a number of science-fiction films, the best of which is perhaps *Forbidden Planet*. But Robot is not the only man-made thing that provides a source of peril. Even Giant Computer Machines ("Giant Brains", as they are called) have been pictured as developing a will of their own and turning against their creators.

These categories have existed almost ever since science fiction attained sophistication, around the early forties. But this genre of films has never been widely popular, except when done on a big scale with considerable fanfare — as with *War of the Worlds*, *Forbidden Planet* and Disney's *20,000 Leagues Under the Sea*. Modest, imaginative films have been made alongside these, but their very scale has suggested that the makers had been aware of the risks involved.

It seems, however, that a time has come at last when science-fiction films will be looked upon as no bigger risks than, say, a "thriller". Not only that, the genre has started attracting directors who could hardly be associated with frivolous pursuits. Truffaut, and Godard in France, Joseph Losey and Stanley Kubrick in the USA, are either making or have already made their first science-fiction films. Kubrick's film, called *2001: A Space Odyssey*, is being shot in a British studio. I was able to watch a day's work on it last July in the company of Arthur Clarke, astronomer, Kalinga Prize winner and science-fiction writer, who is the co-author of *A Space Odyssey* with Kubrick.

The amount of research that has gone into the film is fantastic. Clarke has made sure that nothing goes into the film that is not scientifically accurate. Thousands of sketches, plans and diagrams of space suits, rockets, moon buses and satellite stations fill the shelves and drawers, and strew the floors of the dozen or so offices of the MGM studio where the film is being shot. One large room is given over to models — of spaceships, landing stations, and satellites. The systematic thoroughness of the whole undertaking has to be seen to be believed. Since the story involves a trip to the moon, a rocket constitutes one of its most important elements. I met the designer of the rocket. He turned out to be one of the top men in the field of actual rocket designing. In other words, the rocket used in the film was theoretically capable of making actual space flights, although it never had to leave the studio floor.

Kubrick at his office during the shooting of *2001: A Space Odyssey*. Photograph by Satyajit Ray

When I arrived on the set, a shot was being taken of the control panel of the rocket. For this purpose, sixteen 16 mm cameras had been set up behind the control board, and were simultaneously projecting sixteen animated charts in colour to sixteen viewing panels on the board. And these are the panels which the 70 mm camera was photographing. Clarke said that all those charts would make sense to a scientist.

Both the meticulousness and the scale seemed to uphold the claim of the makers of *A Space Odyssey*, that this was going to be the biggest film ever made. And biggest naturally also means the costliest.

As I left the studio that evening, I really had the feeling that science fiction was coming into its own at last; and that whatever else the future may hold for mankind, it certainly holds the promise of better and more serious science-fiction films.

AN APPRECIATION OF SILENT FILMS

Lecture given at the History of Motion Picture symposium at the American University Center, Kolkata, June 1967

We all know that extraordinary things have happened in the cinema world during the last ten to fifteen years. We know of the emergence of new schools and new styles in film-making, of the new permissiveness that marks the content of the modern films of the West as well as the East. We know of the new wave that has left behind the legacy of unshackled film-making. We know of the American underground and we also know of the collapse of the tried and true Hollywood system of big film production, perhaps the most striking and significant event of all.

But in addition to all this, one must note another recent phenomenon. This has nothing to do with film-making but with film appreciation. This is the sudden upsurge of interest in the beginnings of the cinema brought about by a steady stream of revivals of silent films in the archives and cinematheques of the world.

A great deal of fresh thinking on the art of the cinema has resulted from this. What was once patrionisingly thought of as rudimentary and backward has now emerged as valid achievements in an independent and self-sufficient art form.

Today, one actually wonders whether the introduction of words into films was not, in fact, introduction of an impurity undermining the direct visual impact of the medium. There is no denying the fact that with the coming of sound, images in films became, in general, less meaningful in themselves. After all with sound and with words, one can always fall back on words to convey one's meaning.

A great many of the sound films made in the heyday of talkies now seem dated, not just because of the weight of words but because of the texture of their visual style. In the period I have in mind, the star system was at its height. This meant a cautious approach on the part of everybody concerned in the making of a film. Because what was at stake, above all, was the image of the star.

Portrait of Chaplin drawn by Ray

Now this is a state of affairs that didn't exist in the silent era. The true stars were then the makers of the films themselves — the directors. Of course, it was not uncommon for leading actors to take to directing their own films. Many of the great slapstick comedians used to do it. But these star directors never lost sight of the importance of the ensemble. One has only to look at a Chaplin shot to see how perfectly the small parts are cast and played.

The film-makers of the silent days worked much harder and much longer on their films than their modern counterparts.

Often they worked just for the love of it with humility and with no hope of rewards or of the kind of adulation that is showered upon some of the luminaries of the present time. In consequence of this, sadly enough, many of these artists along with their works passed quickly into oblivion.

No one has done more to try and rescue them than Kevin Brownlow. In addition to being a film-maker, Brownlow was a collector of silent movies. And the more he collected, the more his conviction grew that there were many directors, many actors and many technicians of the silent period, who had not been given due recognition by film historians. So Brownlow set about hunting down these figures from the past in the United States as well as in other parts of the world and talking to them and getting them to talk about their work.

SILENT F

An Appreciation by S~

Among Indian film makers, Satyajit Ray stands in a class by himself. His films have attained international renown. His Pather Panchali (1955), the first part of a trilogy on a popular Bengali novel, won the Cannes Film Festival award in 1956 for "best human document." The second in the trilogy, Aparajita, won the Grand Prix at the Venice Film Festival in 1957. Altogether the trilogy (Apur Sansar was the third) has won 16 international awards. In 1967 Ray was honoured with the Magsaysay Award for the Communication Arts. This Appreciation is taken from a lecture he gave at the History of Motion Picture symposium at the American University Centre, Calcutta, in June.

We all know that extraordinary things have happened in the cinema world during the last ten to fifteen years. We know of the emergence of new schools and new styles in film making, of the new permissiveness that marks the content of the modern films of the West as well as the East. We know of the new wave that has left behind the legacy of unshackled film making. We know of the American underground and we also know of the collapse of the tried and true Hollywood system of big film production, perhaps the most striking and significant event of all.

But in addition to all this one must note another recent phenomenon. This has nothing to do with film making but with film appreciation. This is the sudden upsurge of interest in the beginnings of the cinema brought about by a steady stream of revivals of silent films in the archives and cinematheques of the world.

A great deal of fresh thinking on the art of the cinema has resulted from this. What was once patronisingly thought of as rudimentary and backward has now emerged as valid achievements in an independent and self-sufficient art form.

Today, one actually wonders whether the introduction of words into films was not in fact introduction of an impurity undermining the direct visual impact of the medium. There is no denying the fact that with the coming of sound, images in films became, in general, less meaningful in themselves. After all with sound and with words, one can always fall back on words to convey one's meaning.

A great many of the sound films made in the heyday of talkies now seem dated, not just because of the weight of words but because of the texture of their visual style.

Their life span as a popular art was short, less than 30 years. But the Silent Film as an art form, a medium of creative expression, remains. Each year the Museum of Modern Art, New York, makes available to film clubs and art groups of many countries these original classics. Here are scenes from films that will be shown in India this winter. And 'The American Reporter' is especially pleased to have as its guest Producer Satyajit Ray with 'An Appreciation.'

Charlie Chaplin and Jackie Coogan in "The Kid" (1921). Chaplin ranks as the international screen's greatest comedian — if not its greatest artist. He is one of the few who made the successful transition from silent to sound films.

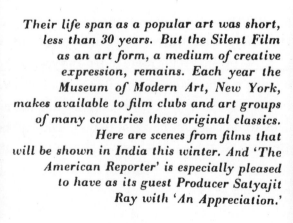

Rudolph V
rocketed th
until his c

IT RAY

The four early greats of the Triangle Film Corporation that set out to capture for the film the prestige and respectability of the stage. From left to right: Thomas Ince, Charlie Chaplin, Mack Sennett, and D.W. Griffith.

...he star system was at its height. This meant a cautious ...body concerned in the making of a film. Because what ...e image of the star.

...fairs that didn't exist in the silent era. The true stars ...films themselves—the directors. Of course, it was ...ctors to take to directing their own films. Many of ...used to do it. But these star-directors never lost sight ...ble. One has only to look at a Chaplin shot to see ...are cast and played

...silent days worked much harder and much longer on ...counterparts.

...for the love of it with humility and with no hope of ...ation that is showered upon some of the luminaries of ...nce of this, sadly enough, many of these artists along ...y into oblivion.

...to try and rescue them than Kevin Brownlow. In ...er, Brownlow was a collector of silent movies. And ...re his conviction grew that there were many directors, ...ians of the silent period, who had not been given due ... So Brownlow set about hunting down these figures ...ates as well as in other parts of the world and talking ...talk about their work.

...he most important film books of our time — The ...ich forces a revision of the conventional attitude ...n the text, which is crammed with fascinating reve-...s in the book have incredible things to tell us about ...in those days, about the wonderful feeling for light ...eramen had and about the meticulous work of the

...es of that period such as the Fairbanks films or ...Notre Dame are far superior visually to their present-...ounterparts, simply because better testing and better ...esigning. In fact, the key figures of the silent period

...deed a unique and self-sufficient art form which was ...mmercial pressures with the coming of sound. It is a ...artists ceased to be, but because forces stronger than ...unction. The least we can do as lovers of the cinema, ...ated, to as many of these artists as we can and make ...torian's neglect of them.

...Gone By.. " is available on loan from all American Libraries

Harold Lloyd in a scene from "Never Weaken" (1921). He was always trying to get out of trouble in unusual and harrowing situations. Along with Charlie Chaplin, Buster Keaton and Harry Langdon, Lloyd formed the band of the great comedians of the silent era.

...Terry in "The Four Horsemen of the Apocalypse" (1921), the film that ...r to stardom. Valentino became the romantic idol of millions of women ...y an early death.

Douglas Fairbanks with Enid Bennett in "Robin Hood" (1922). Fairbanks, another matinee idol of the silent era, is the archetypal swash-buckling romantic hero upon which Tyrone Power and Errol Flynn were later modelled. Fairbanks made 43 films between 1915 and 1932.

The result was one of the most important film books of our time — *The Parade's Gone By*, which forces a revision of the conventional attitude to silent cinema. Apart from the text, which is crammed with fascinating revelations, the hundreds of stills in the book have incredible things to tell us about the quality of camera work in those days, about the wonderful feeling for light and landscape that these cameramen had and about the meticulous work of the set designers.

Some of the big spectacles of that period such as the Fairbanks films or *Ben-Hur* or *The Hunchback of Notre Dame* are far superior visually to their present-day Panavision technicolour counterparts, simply because better testing and better research had gone into their designing. In fact, the key figures of the silent period were all perfectionists.

The silent cinema was indeed a unique and self-sufficient art form which was wiped out of existence by commercial pressures with the coming of sound. It is a vanished art not because the artists ceased to be, but because forces stronger than theirs willed and planned its extinction. The least we can do as lovers of the cinema, is to pay homage, however belated, to as many of these artists as we can and make amends for the nearsighted historian's neglect of them.

THE TREASURE OF SIERRA MADRE (1948)

Programme note written by Ray for Cine Club of Calcutta, 8 January 1970

Poster of *The Treasure of Sierra Madre*

Director: John Huston; **Screenplay:** John Huston; **Photography:** Ted McCord; **Music:** Max Steiner; **Producer:** Henry Blanke; **Players:** Humphrey Bogart, Walter Huston, Tim Holt, Bruce Bennett, Barton MacLane, Alfonso Bedoya

Awards: Academy Awards, New York Film Critics' Awards, National Board of Review, International Prize for Best Music.

John Huston's *The Treasure of Sierra Madre* (1948) represents one of the high points in the peak period in Hollywood's history, the forties. Huston himself — on the strength of just one film — *The Maltese Falcon* — was already a figure to reckon with; a director with a remarkable confident style, tough, economical, and with a superb control over actions. *Sierra Madre* shows all these qualities, plus a touch of poetry which arises out of the subject itself.

B. Traven's book describes what happens to a trio of down-and-outs in Mexico who go searching for gold in the mountains. The story starts with two of them (played by Humphrey Bogart and Tim Holt) hanging around in the sweltering heat of a small Mexican town looking for a job. They get a job in a construction site but are cheated out of their payment. In a savage, superbly shot scene, they beat up the foreman in a bar while electric fans slowly rotate overhead. Later, they meet the old bum (a memorable performance by the director's father Walter Huston) who leads them to the gold. The greater part of the film is concerned with the tense psychological interplay between the three characters as they slowly crack up under the strain of mutual suspicion.

Huston has made many films since *Sierra Madre*, but none with quite the same momentous simplicity of this one. It is interesting to note that Huston's three best films (*Sierra Madre*, *Maltese Falcon* and *African Queen*) were all made with Humphrey Bogart.

ON SCRIPT WRITING

Published in *St. Xavier's College Magazine*, 1970

FILM DIRECTION AND SCRIPT WRITING

When I started making films, I felt that the greatest weakness of the Bengali cinema was the scenario. I think the situation has not changed much since then. Of course, there are a few exceptions; among Bengali film-makers, Ritwik Ghatak and Mrinal Sen have directed films which contain long stretches of great excellence.

The artistic mind, in India, is not used to the idea of unchangeable formal structure existing in time. Our principal art form is music, and our music is improvised. A musical performance can last anything from one to three hours, according to the musician's mood. But you can't make a film like that. Many of our novels have not the type of structure you can analyse. The novel *Pather Panchali*, for instance, is discursive, episodic. It is almost too life-like in its rhythms and pace. There have been some remarkably structured novels made by men like Bankim Chandra, Manik Banerjee and Tagore, occasionally. But the general tendency is a kind of episodic, discursive approach to story telling, and this has never worked in the case of films. As a result our films have remained shapeless and unsatisfactory.

The cinema was born in the West, and there has always been a deep affinity between the cinema and Western musical tradition. It is significant that most of the great pioneers of the cinema were musically conscious. Think, for instance, of Griffith, who was constantly referring to Beethoven, and of Eisenstien. Western music has definitely had some influence in the evolution of the form of the film in the West. Now we don't have that kind of tradition here. In my own case, from the age of fifteen, I have been familiar with Western music, the sonata form, the whole classical school and the romantics. I think one has to have this feeling of a pattern existing in time, a pattern which can be comprehended only over a period of time, which is rigid, unchangeable, and which has a satisfying shape and rhythm.

In the West, and even here, directors rarely write their own scripts, with the exception of men like Bergman, Fellini, Antonioni and few others. Most directors who write their own scripts employ writers for the dialogue. In my view, a director should be his own scriptwriter. For, after the basic conception, the primary composition is the scenario, and if somebody else writes the scenario for the director, that part of the credit for the complete film should go to the scenario writer.

Some film-makers may give the impression that they do not use a script and improvise. In fact, one never knows whether a film is improvised or not. The director may have given certain scenes a great deal of thought at home. It may not be on paper, but this comes to the same thing. Even if you do improvise, the moment you set the camera, you stop improvising. You can tell your actors to improvise their dialogue; but you're not necessarily going to keep everything in. You are going to cut something out. At some point or the other, you're introducing a certain element of order into your material.

Whether it comes before you start shooting or at the time of editing can make some difference, but not a great one. Griffith never had a written scenario. He always had it in his head. He knew what he was going to do. Of course, you can do that. You can even go with a blank mind and do anything you like. (I have seen ostensibly improvised films like *Shadows* by John Cassavetes.) I would not mind doing this once in a while to see what you can achieve, but this can be very costly.

SCRIPT WRITING FOR ME

I have been writing my own scenarios ever since I started making films. Even before I made my first film, I used to write screenplays as a pastime. I would take up a novel which had been announced for filming by somebody else, write a treatment of that, and compare it with the film. I found this most instructive. It has been, and it remains, an absolute necessity for me to work on a script. In the case of *Pather Panchali*, I did not have a script, really speaking, but it was all in my head.

In the old days, say up to *Charulata*, I always went out of town to write my scenarios. I used to go to a lonely seaside place — may be Gopalpur or Puri. There, I worked alone, without any assistance, with not even my wife and son to accompany me. In such lonely places, I work much quicker and can produce much more work. I can keep at it sixteen or seventeen hours a day. Of course, when I left, I knew what story I wanted to make into a film. I never took longer than ten days to write a scenario. After that, there remained only to brush up and improve the dialogue. Nowadays I am getting used to the noise here. Somehow I can cut it off.

One of the reasons why I have written my scripts from the very first film, is that I could not think of anyone I could turn to. And in the beginning, I would not have thought of making a film without a script. Even now, I prefer to write my own scenarios for various reasons: first, I have an orderly method of work, that is, my mind works like that; secondly, you spend more money if you don't have a script, and you can't afford that.

My shooting ratio for *Pather Panchali* was seven to one. It was only two and a half to one in *Kanchenjunga*. That was the lowest ratio I ever achieved. My usual ratio is about four to one. But *Kanchenjunga* was in colour, therefore more expensive, so I was more disciplined; and also, I had very fine actors, among whom was the late Chhabi Biswas, an old-timer. The actors had learned their lines and were ready when they faced the camera. The new actors, also, were wonderful.

I once read an interview of Antonioni in which he said with some satisfaction, that his ratio was ten to one. In fact, one would not mind shooting a high ratio of footage to get the kind of perfection one wants. But sometimes you just have to stop, for other considerations. If, however, it is something which, if not perfect, would really matter, then you go on shooting until you get it. I had to go up to ten or twelve takes for a correct synchronization of movements in *Pather Panchali*.

We had a shot where Apu and his sister, Durga, start running after a candyman, a confectioner. In the shot where they first spot the candyman, the children were seen in the foreground. Behind them, in the background, was a dog. The children had to run and go out of frame while the camera kept on shooting at the dog. Someone was supposed to call him. But he was an untrained dog and would not go at the right time. So we kept trying again and again. There is no cut there in the finished film. It had to be in one shot, otherwise it would not be interesting. In the same shot, the dog gets up and follows the children who follow the candyman, and, in a later shot, their reflection is seen in a pond. I had one of the children put his hand behind his back, holding some sweets. So the dog followed them.

My method of work has grown out of certain considerations. We operate in a very small market and we have a very special kind of audience. In my case, the potential audience is even smaller because I make very personal films, sometimes rather serious films, and they are always somewhat different from the usual run of films. And yet, you make films first for your own audience. I cannot ignore my audience here. My audience means not only the audience in the city, but also in the suburbs, the lowest common denominator. The problem is to make a film that they will not entirely reject, and at the same time, one that will be accepted at Venice, Cannes or Berlin, and later on also in Europe generally. This is a very sophisticated audience. If I ignored either of them, I could be freer. If I ignored my audience here and made films only for the West, if I made them, as subtle as possible, if I treated more difficult subjects, more adult, let's say more frank, more sophisticated, more complex subjects, then I would be doing different films, taking up different stories.

Besides, when you make films, most of the time you are using somebody else's money. Immediately certain responsibilities come to you. You are always waiting for the next man to come to offer you the required money. When one comes, you realize that this man is investing lots of money which he hopes to get back. So I generally tell my producers beforehand what to expect from my films. When I made *Charulata*, I told my producer: "This film may win prizes abroad, but I don't know if you will make a profit out of it." He said: "I don't mind, I like the story, make it." But if he had said: "No." I would not have made the film. I made it very clear in other cases also, like that of *Devi*. In the case of *Jalsaghar*, I told my producer: "This is going to be a fairly important film, I think. You may find a market abroad, but I don't know about my own audience here, because they have not been tested."

OVER THE YEARS

My method has not changed very much, except that over the years I have acquired a certain proficiency. Basically I think the process has remained more or less the same: first the outline, then the breakdown.

Writing the dialogue has improved enormously, I think one always overwrites at the beginning. Even now, I find occasionally — not as frequently as before — when a scene is being shot, that they're talking too much. Maybe a gesture here, a gesture there, will take the place of words which you can drop. The general tendency is to overwrite, to put too much. That's because your visual imagination is not working to the same extent while you are writing. You have to get into a state where you just live the scenes and imagine the actors living them, surrounded by the props in this or that location, getting up moving about. Generally, when you start writing dialogues, you imagine the actors are just talking, which is not the case. That's why I never rehearse, except on location, or, in the studio, when the set is ready with all the props and everything, so that I know precisely how the actors will move, what they will do, etc. In fact, every action affects the words. Sometimes your mind is distracted momentarily and you repeat something you said just before. And so, everything in the scene, in the shot, has to be taken into consideration, even the season of the year, because, for instance, in winter you talk in a different way from summer. You're more relaxed at certain times. Your state of mind, the props surrounding you and the business that you're performing, whether you are just sitting idly or active in some work, all this makes for different types of dialogue. So, I think my dialogue is becoming more and more life-like. This is not naturalism, but a kind of selective realism, which works only for a particular scene and with a dialogue the actors find very easy to say. I have discovered that a dialogue which is easy to speak improves the acting, because the actors know that what they are saying comes naturally and not like rhetorical speech.

I have also made progress with regard to the structure of my films. For instance, in *Pather Panchali* and in *Aparajito*, there were things which had to be cut out at the stage of editing. These things seemed redundant, or weak and unnecessary. That would obviously mean that the script was not perfectly conceived. On the other hand, in some cases, I could shoot only parts of some scenes because of lack of money, so the unprinted bits had to be left out. Some of these were very good scenes. Had they been completed, they'd be in the finished film. But they were not. The trilogy had a very special character in the sense that it was not a story: it had a kind of biographical quality to it, and this needed a different kind of script. If you had a plotted structure, that would need another approach. Since the trilogy, I have not attempted anything on the same lines, that is, a film with the quality of a biography, with the flow and rhythm of life rather than that of a plotted story.

HOW I WRITE A SCRIPT

If I am working on somebody else's story, then to write the script means, first of all, casting the story into the form of a film. It then becomes a slightly different story, with a different rhythm and a different sequence of events to it, unless the original story happened to be very close to a film treatment, which is very rarely the case. So, often there is a considerable degree of adaptation which is required, and I do that adaptation. I cast the story in the form of a screen-story. But this is never for me a literary effort. It's something that I have to do, which I wish I did not have to do. Anyway, it's a form of writing, which I don't think of as a literary effort at all. It's just a kind of an outline — a block treatment, as the term goes — and as brief as possible.

In script writing, everything works as long as the final product is satisfactory. I don't think you can frame strict rules any more. A certain degree of grammar is necessary, and you learn that by looking at films more than anything else. That's the way we learned. We used to go to movies which we liked, even to movies we did not like, more than once

— the bad movies, to see what was wrong with them, but the good movies we could see five, six, or seven times. I even started at one time to take notes in the dark. But when it actually comes to shooting your own films, all that may be at the back of your mind, but I think your style, your editing method, your set-ups are all dictated by your material. You are not applying rules there. The material of your story, of your subject matter, guides you. Such rules as "don't cut from extreme long shot to close-up", all that is gone. Nobody takes that seriously anymore, because emotional continuity is much more important than continuity of external movement.

I visualize everything very clearly, so all I have to do is to convey what I have in mind. Often, I express it pictorially. This is essential. I think that all the directors who have a sufficient degree of control over their material do the same thing. I do small sketches for my shots. That is the final stage of shooting the script. This is not a typewritten thing which I distribute to my crew. It's a series of drawings of shots, with notes on the dialogue and camera movement. It also shows the frame and the magnification. That is good for discussion with the art director and the cameraman.

Music does not come right at the beginning. But at the time of writing the scenario, I become aware of certain situations. I know I might need music. If a certain theme or motif presents itself, I note it down in my script, sometimes in the margin. Suddenly a line of melody comes and strikes me that it would suit a certain situation. I generally use music in a leitmotif sort of fashion. It's not a new piece of music for every situation, but it rises out of certain thematic material. It maybe one or two main themes. Then I produce variations on them, like in the film *Charulata*. This process is very clear there. I also have a separate notebook with staff notation. In that book I keep noting down themes, not necessarily for a particular film, but for some film in the future. These are just musical ideas. They are usually fragments of melody, sometimes with notes on the instruments which would probably be most appropriate, for a melody is not suitable for all instruments. Sometimes the idea comes only as a brave line of melody, sometimes it comes dressed in a certain orchestral colour.

Shatranj — Introduction

Page from hand-written scenario of *Shatranj Ke Khilari*

SQ 1   SCENE I

The Residency. General Outram's Study. Afternoon.

Outram ~~has a paper in his hand~~ ...

sits in his chair & reads out from a paper.

Out 'His Majesty listened to a new Singh, and
amused himself afterwards by flying' cute
        in the town of the bulbul
His Majesty wanted a new poem of a Mushaira

What is a Mushaira, Weston?'

Wes It's a gathering of poets, sir. They recite
their new poems.

Out A chorus?

Wes No, sir, singly.

Out Him ... 'Diwan Khan, keeper of the pigeon house' isn't it?
received a Khilat' — which means a reward,
Wes Yes sir
    ' a Khilat of Rs 2000 for producing
a pigeon with one white and one black wing'
My dear, why did the ...
...

Outram throws the paper aside. His mind ... of the King's
doings, Outram he leans back in his chair, chewing his
cheroot, ... a deep frown ...
his brow furrowed by a deep frown. Weston gives a
short cough.

Wes There is a
    A dispatch from General Wheler ...
    Sir. The troops arrived in Cawnpore
    ... orders
    & are awaiting orders, ... to march
    into Lucknow.

Outram is absentmindedly. There is something on his mind.
He speaks after an appreciable pause

Page from hand-written scenario of *Shatranj Ke Khilari*

THE BREAKDOWN

The breakdown has to be planned very carefully: which scene to shoot first, which set, location to shoot first. It is a fairly elaborate thing: there is the question of finding the right locations, of discussing with the art director what sets to build, the question of the available date of the studios if you are going to shoot in a studio. If it is entirely on location, as in *Pather Panchali*, we have to find a location, we have to find actors, and then we decide on the manner of shooting, which scene to tackle first, etc. Then, I start doing the breakdown in terms of shots. With the location work, this is kept fairly flexible, because one always gets ideas on location. You change your camera viewpoint, you change for better light; suddenly a breeze blows and you perceive a better angle for a certain shot, so you change the angle. Sometimes you do tracking shots instead of static shots, or vice versa, depending on how your trolly is functioning. If it's giving trouble, then one long tracking shot can be broken up on the spot into five shots.

Shooting in the studio becomes a more rigid affair, because you have the sets there: you usually, have only three walls to them, so your angles are limited; you have to light up for a certain angle and then finish that angle and go on the next one.

In my script, I also leave room for improvisations in the dialogue. If you're working with non-professional actors, sometimes certain words, certain lines of dialogue don't come naturally to them, so you constantly modify; you simplify; you increase or decrease the number of words.

FROM STORY TO SCREENPLAY

Sometimes, in the process of turning a story into a screenplay, I find that certain characters begin to change. Then script writing becomes a process of criticism of the original, because, as you think deeply about the lines of development, some characters do not seem any more to behave in a convincing manner. So then starts a process of modification and the conclusion becomes slightly different from that of the original story. This happens all the time. Sometimes you discover a serious basic flaw in the original story and you abandon the whole thing because it is not what you had thought it was. It has happened once or twice in my experience — not recently though, earlier on. Something which I had read years ago, and which had struck me as a wonderful story, I would read it again and start treating it in terms of a screenplay. Then I'd find that there were flaws in it, which, maybe, the original author did not notice or which you don't mind in a literary work. But in a film everything is more concrete, and the time span is so brief and continuous that you are more alert somehow, and therefore, certain things strike you as being wrong, or maybe, not quite properly drawn.

If a story once read sticks in the mind, I usually read it again. It is usually in the second reading that the real worth of a story as film material emerges. If I begin to see the sweep of the film in it, a third reading usually helps make up my mind. After that, I never touch the story again. I even forget it sometimes. It doesn't matter to me whether I am departing from the original, even if it is a hallowed Tagore story.

Sometimes the whole story, with everything in it, stays in your mind; then, of course, it's already almost a film and you don't have to work so hard. But you still have to find the cinematic equivalent of certain literary things. In *Charulata*, the first seven or eight minutes of loneliness correspond to twenty pages of writing. I could see that the essential thing to establish in the beginning was the loneliness of Charulata. But what is loneliness? Loneliness is lack of company, which means lack of communication. One has to find the cinematic equivalent of Charulata's loneliness. Without taking recourse to commentary or words just show her loneliness: what can a lonely woman do? How does she spend her time? Is she still useful? There are two kinds of loneliness: the loneliness of old age, and the loneliness of youth when there is still the desire for company. So this was the initial situation in *Charulata* and I worked on that. It did not matter to me at all that I was omitting the first twenty pages of Tagore, because I knew I had the substance. This is what I had to establish in order that the rest might follow logically: the coming of the brother-in-law, the falling in love, the husband, etc.

Even with that kind of freedom in adapting, at the time the film is finished, I know I have made a story by Tagore into a film. It is an interpretation, a "trans-creation" not a translation. Without Tagore, there would be no *Charulata*. After all, he set me off, he was the reason for it. There is a lot of the original in the film. A certain state of mind which the author describes beautifully with words … you can't do that in films. You have to use a different method. Tagore is a great poet, a great writer. He uses wonderful language to describe loneliness and all the small things that go on in the mind. All the time, you have to find something for Charulata to do to establish her state of mind. That is the challenge of the cinema.

Now, when you take up a story, you do not necessarily like the whole of it. Maybe, one strong situation or certain things strike you which you want to put into film. But if you were to do an original story and use these situations or things, you would be plagiarizing. So you get in touch with the author and tell him, "I'm going to make a film of your story and I'm going to do my own treatment. I am going to make the necessary modification". He agrees and he is paid for it. He sells the rights. In *Mahanagar*, a lot of things in the original story come in the film. But it is a short story to begin with, so you start developing it. You start from the situation which fascinated you in the beginning: the wife having to go out and work to add to the family's income. That's your starting point. And then, of course, you have the inevitable psychological development of husband and wife suddenly feeling this situation; of the husband's feeling of inferiority, with all the psychological complications this involves, and then the child, and the conservative parents. These elements are all in the original story.

Certain stories of Tagore are quite Victorian in their feeling. Take "Postmaster": at the end of the original story, the postmaster is supposed to leave and the little servant girl falls at his feet and says, "Please don't leave me alone, please, take me with you." This struck me as being sentimental. I could not express that because it was an emotion I don't feel, being a man of the twentieth-century, being brought up in certain surroundings, being exposed to certain influences. So, I made the ending of the story more dry, yet moving in its own way. I made it into the opposite of what it was. The girl in the film hides her grief instead of displaying it. She ignores the postmaster. She is so hurt that she does not even want to tell this man that she is unhappy. You see her weeping by the well from which she is drawing water. But the moment he calls her she wipes her tears. She walks past him carrying the bucket of water and ignores the tip that he was about to offer her. That was my interpretation as a twentieth-century artist working in 1960. The purists object to these changes. Well, I made them because I also am an artist with my own feelings. I was using Tagore's rendering of a story as a basis, and this was my interpretation of it.

There are other similar changes in my other films — in the Apu trilogy, for instance. The trilogy was not originally planned by me as a trilogy. When I made *Pather Panchali*, I had no idea of making *Aparajito*, because, at that time, I could not think beyond one film. There was no knowing how the public would react. After the success of *Pather Panchali*, I thought of making the second part. Even then, there was no question of the third part. *Aparajito* was followed by *Jalsaghar* and *Paras Pathar*. Only after *Aparajito* won the Venice prize did I suddenly think of making a third Apu film. When I made *Aparajito*, I naturally had *Pather Panchali* in mind, but they were not meant to be seen in a single programme, as a totality, as a six-hour-long epic. But I used certain recurring symbols, like the train, and the musical motifs of *Pather Panchali* come back in *Aparajito* and also in *Apur Sansar*.

At the end of *Pather Panchali*, a snake is seen crawling into the deserted house of Apu's family. That snake is not in the book. I needed something more than just the family leaving. I wanted to stress the fact that the house was deserted. I could simply have shown the house with no people around, but the snake entering the house clinches the matter.

In *Apur Sansar* when Apu learns of his wife's death, he hits his brother-in-law who has just delivered the news to him. That needed some thought, because I was trying to put myself in the place of Apu. I was not familiar with such a situation in real life. It was difficult to tell what would happen, and the more deeply I thought about it, the more I felt that, for a man like Apu, it was natural suddenly to hit the person who brought him such bad news. It seemed to me a psychologically convincing thing to do. As this does not occur in the book, this part of my film was strongly criticized. I thought the criticism ridiculous, I was myself convinced that the gesture was the correct one, and my actor shared my conviction.

THE CHOICE OF SOME OF MY STORIES

The Three Daughters was undertaken as a tribute to Tagore. It was his centenary year. I had made the Tagore documentary, and I thought I should do some short stories as well. I did *Monihara*, the ghost story, because I am very fond of ghost stories. Of course, you would not do a ghost story today and take it seriously. This is a different age. But then you want to play about with the film medium also, because, after all, you only have one life-time, so you do as much as you can. Not many others do that. Everything has fallen into a rut, so why not explore while there is time for it.

There are only two instances where circumstances forced me to take up a film. *Abhijaan* and *Chiriakhana*, the detective story, were not things of my own choice. There are wonderful aspects of film-making, like working with wonderful actors. If the location is exciting, if you have a good crew, then you are in it in no time. You get involved in it. You enjoy the process of making the film. Then, you forget about whether the story was worth it or not. You give it all you have. Something like this happened in the case of *Abhijaan*. This was based on a novel by Tarashankar Bandyopadhyay. A group of friends wanted to make it into a film. They asked me to write the scenario for them. I did so. Then they asked me to see the locations. I went and found that extraordinary place: an area of one square mile covered with rocks. This was not in the original script. I put it in. Then I helped them to select the spots for shooting. Finally, I took over at their request. I made changes in the scenario and I gave more thought to it, because, at first, it was one of those adventurous, plotty novels, so I could only do this up to a point. Then I concentrated on the acting, because there were acting possibilities in it, and I had wonderful actors, and wonderful locations. Such things are great fun. I love working. I love making films regardless of what I am making.

The rights to make *Chiriakhana* were purchased by some friends and they asked me to help them. It was a weak detective story. Detective stories don't make good films anyway. You only wait for the revelation of "who had done it", and once it comes, there is nothing else; and then at the end you have a long lecture. I don't like detective stories in films. A thriller? Fine, you can create good suspense with that.

Abhijaan and *Chiriakhana* were not of my own selection. I would not have made them anyway. But at the time of *Chiriakhana* I was, myself, in a very awkward position. My producer had just walked off *Goopy Gyne Bagha Byne*: we had recorded the songs, and we went to Rajasthan looking for locations. Suddenly, he was panic-stricken. He said, "No". I was completely left in the lurch with nothing to do, and I don't like to be idle too long. Then there came this offer of a detective story. Again there was an interesting cast, these friends who had purchased the rights of *Chiriakhana* and I just took it over.

THE USE OF COLOUR

If colour could be controlled sufficiently, one would, perhaps, make everything in colour. But colour, in its present state, tends to prettify things a little. Also, you are constricted by the fact that you are using three primary bases. Even if you can control one of them, the others will be producing their natural combinations, which you cannot control. The trouble is that it's not like paint, and that keeps worrying me.

In *Kanchenjunga* I deliberately chose colour, because I felt it would be very interesting. This was a two-hour story with no lapse of time. I had the characters wear the same clothes all the way through. Since they split into groups you had this very interesting effect of having a different colour combination for each group appearing by turns. It works formally. I planned the story in such a way that even the landscape underwent certain natural changes. At one point of the story you have the mist coming in and everything, for a certain length of time, is subdued. You see through the mist, and all the colours are automatically muted. No laboratory tricks are involved here, just nature helping you. Finally, the mist rises, but by that time the sun has gone down. Everything has a kind of reddish glow. (For that part of the film all the scenes were shot after five o' clock.)

The story starts on a sunny day. Then clouds come, the sun is obscured, so that you have another chromatic range altogether. Then, the mist comes, that gives a third quality. Then the mist rises, the clouds go, but the sun is so low that everything is muted again. These changes were wedded to emotional states. The colours of the dresses were chosen very carefully with psychological effect in mind. What sort of colour would this kind of a girl wear on this particular occasion? The two sisters were very differently dressed for psychological reasons. The father had a grey suit and a little red handkerchief sticking out of his pocket, showing his pride, and a yellow walking stick. This film required a tremendous amount of planning. I had a map drawn of the Darjeeling area where we were supposed to shoot. This was included in the script itself, and the various locations were all marked. The time of shooting in each location was also indicated. Suppose we were shooting in location C and suddenly the mist came to location D, we had to run for some shots in the mist there. Everything was within a half-mile radius, and it was planned so as not to waste time. That's why we could shoot 26,000 feet of film in 26 days, shooting every day. So in 26 days, less than a month, shooting of the film was finished.

One does not imagine *Aparajito* in colour. Benaras would be so gorgeous with pretty colours that the whole mood would be destroyed. The director should have the freedom to switch from black and white to colour. Some have done it already. I did it in *Goopy Gyne Bagha Byne*. That was a film of magic. There is a kind of an in-joke when the two princesses refuse to look at the two boys, Bagha and Goopy. The boys were shy, and the princesses probably thought they were ordinary boys. So Bagha had the brilliant idea of turning himself and Goopy into princes. Both clapped their hands and everything turned into colour. Then the girls looked up. This was attractive. They refused to look at black and white, but given colour, they looked. This had some psychological implications.

ON PRATIDWANDI

Published in *Cine Advance*, 1970

For me, *Pratidwandi* will be the fulfillment of a long-cherished wish to film a story of present-day urban youth in the setting of our throbbing metropolis. I had made films about contemporary urban people before, but both *Kanchunjungha* and *Arannyer Dinratri* showed what happens to such people when they are cut off from their normal surroundings. The setting of *Pratidwandi*, however, is emphatically the city of Calcutta — Calcutta as it is today.

Once Sunil Ganguly's story had provided the essential impetus, we decided to boldly face the hazards of shooting on location in the streets of the city. That most of this shooting has already been done with surprising ease is probably because (a) we are using a cast of either completely or comparatively unknown actors and (b) we have been shooting with great speed in mainly non-residential areas.

The events described in the story centre around a young man in search of a job. He is seen in relation to his family (consisting of his widowed mother, his younger brother and younger sister), his two friends, the girl he falls in love with, and finally, but by no means the least importantly, to the city itself. I believe that of all my films, *Pratidwandi* will prove to be the most contemporary in mood, in feeling and in technique.

THE PASSING OF THE ERA OF SILENT FILMS

Keynote address at the inaugural session of "Silent Era Classics" and symposium on "History of the Motion Pictures — USA", American University Centre, Calcutta, 1970. Published in *Amrita Bazar Patrika*, 19 June, 1970

Poster of *Nosferatu*

We all know that extraordinary things have been happening in the cinema during the last ten or fifteen years. We know of the emergence of new schools and new styles in film-making; of the new permissiveness that marks the content of modern films — of the West as well as the Far East. We know of the New Wave, and the legacy of unshackled film-making it has left behind. We know of the American underground, and we also know of the collapse of the tried-and-true Hollywood system of big film production — perhaps the most striking and significant event of all.

But in addition to all this one must note another recent phenomenon. This deals not with film-making, but with film appreciation. This is the sudden upsurge of interest in the beginnings of the cinema brought about by a steady stream of revivals of silent films in the archives and cinematheques of the world. A great deal of fresh thinking on the art of the cinema has resulted from this. What was once patronisingly thought of as rudimentary and backward has now emerged as valid achievements in an independent and self-sufficient art form. An art form with its own special appeal, and its own special aesthetics.

WITH THE COMING OF SOUND

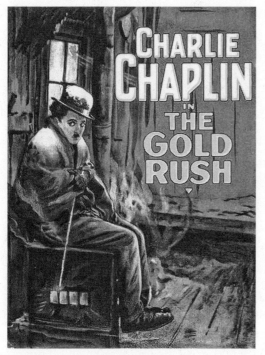

Poster of *The Gold Rush*

Today, one can actually question whether the introduction of words into films was not in fact an introduction of impurity, undermining the direct visual impact of the medium. There is no denying the fact that with the coming of sound, images in films became, in general, less meaningful in themselves. After all, with sound, one can always fall back on words to convey one's meaning. When Chaplin eats his shoes in *The Gold Rush*, he performs an act which is not only funny because of its absurdity; it is also rich with overtones of symbolical meaning, conveyed by purely visual means. The shoe-eating, and all the meaning that goes into it, could never have been conceived in literary terms. And yet, when Chaplin himself — in a literary mood — indulges in metaphysical pronouncements in *Monsieur Verdoux* and *Limelight,* he conveys less sense in a less purely artistic manner, than in that single bit of business with the shoe in *The Gold Rush.*

It is not as if sound films don't contain moments of purely visual significance. But whenever they do, they inevitably hark back to the silent cinema; and more often than not, they prove to be the moments that stay in the mind longest.

HEALTHY TENDENCY

There is a healthy tendency these days to try and restore the purity of the medium lost in the deluge of words; or, in other words, to find one's way back to the original sources of inspiration. This sort of thing has happened at various times in the other arts too.

Many composers have recharged their batteries by going to the sources of folk music; Picasso sought and found inspiration in Negro sculpture; likewise, for any modern film-maker to study the works of the so-called American primitives is bound to prove stimulating.

The achievements of the sound cinema are, of course, considerable. It is possible for a director who is conscious of the silent heritage, to strike a satisfactory balance between sound and image. Words, too, have a valid function to perform. When written by a gifted screen-writer, and spoken by an able actor, words can achieve a certain plastic quality which gives them a significance that is more cinematic than literary. But when an image or an action speaks for itself, it acquires a level of significance in its context which no spoken words can reach. The best of the Westerns made in Hollywood, some superior thrillers, some comedies, some of the bucolic idylls of the French Realist schools, the best of the Japanese and the early Russian schools, and the best of the modern European works, have moments in them which hold one spellbound because they themselves rise above the level of mere verbal speech, and speak through their images.

Even the trend set by Godard in recent times is a predominantly visual one. The words here are often banal, and just as often improvised. This is Godard's way of emphasizing his images, which often acquire a peculiar density though being charged with all manner of contemporary overtones.

WHAT THE STAR SYSTEM DID

A great many of the sound films made in the heyday of talkies now seem dated, not just because of the weight of words, but because of the texture of their visual style. In the period I have in mind, the star system was at its height. This meant a cautious approach on the part of everybody concerned in the making of a film, because what was at stake, above all, was the image of the star. A phrase used to be current in Hollywood in those days: Go for the money. If the cameraman had problems in lighting a set involving a large number of actors in movement, he would be told to "go for the money." So would the focus puller, who wanted to know where to keep his focus. Go for the money. In other words, concentrate on the star, keep your lights on the star, and to hell with the rest. This gave rise to the glamorous school of film craftsmanship. What it did, basically, was to encourage the softening of contours and not only the contours of the star's face, but of the face of the story as well. Take the safe path, take no risks; people don't want to see hard lines on the face of their idols, and a story with hard lines doesn't make for entertainment.

TRUE STARS THEN

Now, this is a state of affairs that didn't exist in the silent era. The true stars then were the makers of the films themselves — the directors. Of course, it was not uncommon for leading actors to take to directing their own films. Many of the great slapstick comedians used to do it. But these star-directors never lost sight of the ensemble. One has only to look at a Chaplin short to see how perfectly the small parts are cast and played.

The film-makers of the silent days worked much harder and much longer on their films than their modern counterparts. There were several reasons for this. First — the apparatus. As compared with modern ones, the old tools were cumbersome. But this doesn't mean that they were inefficient or imperfect. It is a demonstrable fact that the ancient handcranked cameras produced sharper images than the modern portable Arriflexes and Camioflexes. This is because being at least four times heavier, these old cameras were at least four times prone to vibration than the modern ones.

The second reason was that the film-makers had to grapple with a language that was in the process of being evolved — by the makers themselves. This meant that there were far fewer clichés to fall back upon. The director was thus forced to be creative and inventive. And observant too, because, since the camera had to do with reality as it is perceived through the eyes, the director had to rediscover the meanings contained in gestures and in the concrete details of the surroundings.

NOT EXAGGERATED

It is a mistake to assume that acting in the silent cinema was exaggerated, so that all one saw was flinging of arms and rolling of eyeballs. The best actors of the silent days used the minimum expressive gestures. Deprived of words, they had naturally to fall back on stylization, but not necessarily of a sort that jarred one's sensibilities. It could be subtle, and it often was subtle — except when the director aimed at larger-than-life effects. Mack Swain — the mountainous villain in Chaplin's films — did roll his eyes, but this was perfectly right in the context of Chaplin's approach.

Yet another reason why the film-makers took longer on their films was because they were not yet under pressures of the sort that plagued later film-makers — no matter how gifted. Pressures of time, pressures of commerce, pressures from the front office. Film-making in the early days was much more of a personal, intimate affair, where the artists worked lovingly and with painstaking care. Often they worked just for love of it with humility, and with no hope of rewards, or of the kind of adulation that is showered upon some of the luminaries of the present time. In consequence of this, sadly enough, many of these artists along with their works, passed quickly into oblivion.

No one has done more to try and rescue them than Kevin Brownlow. In addition to being a film-maker, Brownlow was a collector of silent movies; and the more he collected, the more his conviction grew that there were many actors, and many technicians of the silent period who had not been given due recognition by film historians. So Brownlow set about hunting down these figures from the past, in the United States as well as in other parts of the world, and talking to them and getting them to talk about their work.

The result is one of the most important film books of our time — *The Parades Gone By* — which forces a revision of the conventional attitude to silent cinema. Some of the big spectacles of that period — such as the Fairbanks films, or *Ben-Hur*, or *The Hunchback of Notre Dame* — are far superior visually to their present day Panavision technicolor counterparts, simply because better taste and better research had gone into their designing. In fact, the key figures of the silent period were all perfectionists. Today, the trend is towards a short-hand method of film-making.

GRIFFITH, THE GIANT

Griffith, of course, emerges as the giant that we knew he was from Kevin Brownlow's book. Ambitious, imaginative and immensely hardworking, Griffith was so confident of the validity and self-sufficiency of his art form, that he made the rash prediction that sound on film was not only scientifically impossible, but aesthetically unnecessary. We know that Griffith was responsible for most of the innovations in the film language, but it is necessary to emphasize — and the book does this with great clarity — that all his innovation came about in order to fulfill certain expressive needs.

The most striking of his innovations was the crane shot — or rather, the precursor of the crane shot. This occurs in *Intolerance*. Those who have seen *Intolerance* will know the breathtaking effect of this shot. This is a shot which could only have been conceived by someone who had something new and important to say and was stubborn and inventive enough to devise a way of saying it.

Sound admittedly brought the cinema closer to actuality. I use the word actuality in order to suggest the surface, rather than the substance, of reality. The substance is not necessarily ensured by the addition of sound, or for that matter, of colour. I have seen many modern documentaries on poverty and other social ills which seem less real than, say, *The Kid* or *City Lights*, and no documentary on locomotives or steamships can tell us more about them than Buster Keaton's *The General* and *The Navigator*.

The silent cinema was indeed a unique and self-sufficient art from which was wiped out of existence by commercial pressures with the coming of sound. It is a vanished art

Lobby Card of Buster Keaton's *The General*

not because the artists ceased to be, but because forces stronger than theirs, willed and planned its extinction. The least we can do, as lovers of cinema, is to pay homage, however related, to an historians' neglect of them.

One important detail before I close. The silent film was never meant to be viewed in silence but with the accompaniment of music. The music was actually played on the piano, sometimes on an organ, and on rare occasions, by an orchestra. We remember from our childhood the mellifluous tones of the Wurlitzer organ in the Palace of Varieties — now the Elite Cinema, just as we remember the tinkly pianos in the other cinemas — the Globe, the Elphinstone, the Picture Palace.

MIRACLE IN MILAN (1951)

Programme note written by Ray for Cine Club of Calcutta, 27 September 1970

Directed by: Vittorio De Sica

Miracle in Milan was made at a time when the De Sica–Zavatiini combination had already established itself as a major creative force in world cinema. Much more elaborately conceived and executed than the earlier films, *Miracle in Milan* also marks a generic change for its makers. Zavattini here departs from strict neo-realism and turns to fantasy. But his basic pursuit — namely, the exploration of poverty — remains unchanged. The bleakness of conclusion which marked both *Shoeshine* and *Bicycle Thieves* here is replaced by a magical fairy-tale 'happy' ending where the hobos, deprived of their territory by business tycoons and facing imminent capture by the police, escape by riding away on broomsticks to a land beyond the skies where 'every morning is a god morning'. This being no real solution, the underlying mood may still be said to be pessimistic; because *Miracle in Milan* is no fairy tale happening 'once upon a time' in a never-never land. It is a story set in modern-day Milan, with its trains, streetcars, limousines, factories and stone-faced office blocks.

While one can question the film's success in its transitions from realism to fantasy, there can be no doubt that the first one hour of the film — up to the point where the fantasy begins — *Miracle in Milan* records the summit of achievement for poetic cinema as a whole, and for De Sica in particular.

The story concerns an orphan boy, Toto, discovered in true fairy-tale tradition, in a cabbage patch, by a kindly old lady. Toto is brought up by her, but loses her when still a boy. After a breathtaking scene where Toto follows the hearse in shivering cold through misty, frost-laden streets, Toto is led into an orphanage by two strangers. He comes out as a young man full of trust and bonhomie, greets the first man with a cheery "good morning", and is immediately met with a growled retort: "What's good about it?"

The subsequent scenes show Toto spreading goodwill and cheer in a colony of hobos living in shanties in an open field on the outskirts of Milan. The scenes bristle with details — by turns poignant, funny, grotesque and lyrical. Much of it is extremely funny, in the classical manner of Chaplin and his Tramp. Think of the balloon seller, who is so greedy and famished that that he is borne aloft by the bunch of balloons in his hand. Of course, he has to be kept down by the other hobos stuffing his pockets full of weights.

The trouble begins when oil is struck in the hobos' territory. Big business giants get wind of this and arrive on the scene to strike a bargain with the hobos. What chance has such beggars against crafty Milanese tycoons? The answer is none whatsoever. And this is where fantasy intervenes in the shape of a magic dove.

Miracle in Milan has masterly photography by G.R. Aldo, one of the great cameraman of our times who was killed in a motor car accident some seven or eight years ago. For the trick work, De Sica engaged Ned Mann of Hollywood, whose credits included *Things to Come*. Mann's work here, particularly in the crucial tricks, is unsatisfactory, which is one of the reasons why the fantasy episodes never seem to come up to the level of the rest of the film. As in all of De Sica's early films, Cicognini's music plays a dominant role.

[As an example of De Sica's meticulous — almost miraculous — castings, note the extraordinary resemblance between the boy Toto and the young Toto.]

LETTER TO FILMFARE

Published in *Filmfare*, 25 February 1972

Apropos of Mr. Bikram Singh's recent rejoinder to my article "An Indian New Wave?" and for the benefit of those who, like Mr. Singh, are trying to fathom "what prompted the busy film-maker to spell out, at such length, his views on the new cinema," let me spell out once again, and for the last time, the main points I was trying to stress in my article, adding only a few fresh remarks arising out of Mr. Singh's piece. This, may I add, would not have been necessary had Mr. Singh given more thought to what I had said in stead of wasting his time in the pursuit of ulterior motives.

I was not concerned with an examination of individual Film Finance Corporation (FFC) sponsored films, but with indicating the broad lines of a possible movement.

The only kind of movement worth having is one with the stamina to survive and spread, and make a discernable impact over an area wide enough to make for economic viability.

For this, the film-maker must come armed with a seriousness of approach, and a preparedness to come to terms with Indian traditions.

However revolutionary the first films of Godard and Truffaut might have seemed, the germs of the French New Wave were already present in the works of earlier French masters. In other words, Truffaut and Godard belonged to the mainstream of French cinema, and therefore, were able to make an impact on a wide scale.

India is not France. While it is possible for an Indian director to be wholly responsive to the Godard mould, he is likely to lose contact with the Indian audience, which, in all probability, will not share his response. As such he is unlikely to make any contribution to the movement.

A film in Cannes, or a film in private screening, has at best only a theoretical existence. Its actual life is in the theatre, in the presence of a paying public. A movement needs films that play to such a public, however select. Any film-maker is free to use the narrative devices of post-Godardian cinema (freeze, jumpcut, negative, split screen, et al.), but not at the expense of the narrative, because narrative is at the core of the Indian tradition.

The truly talented director needs no advice and no encouragement. Sooner or later, he will carve out his niche either within a movement or without it, though not without a public that endorses him.

It is the less talented but aspiring director who needs a helping hand. An experienced director can give him that. So can, and so should, an experienced critic. But all Mr. Singh is able to give him is a pat on the back for having avoided the idiot clutches of Hindi cinema.

And yet, with the creative freedom that the FFC set-up allows the director (as against the brain washing constrictions of the commercial set-up), avoiding such clichés is the least he can do. What one needs for any kind of healthy movement, and what needs to be endlessly demanded by responsible critics, are positive virtues. Any film that avoids the idiot cliches and attains positive virtues (narrative strength and clarity, strong acting, imaginative treatment, sound technical qualities) will find its public — quite possibly without the hothouse nourishment of art theatres — and serve as a pointer to a healthy movement.

In the Indian context, such films would surely represent the avant-garde. To use Mr. Singh's words, they would represent "irrepressible rebellions, determined acts of defiance". As a critic, Mr Singh must be aware that even the field of straightforward serious narrative cinema remains virtually unexplored in Hindi films — at least in the last fifteen years or so. It would surely not do to overlook the various stages of growth between crawling and running. After all, the audience grows up with the films, not independently of them.

An avant-garde in the European sense would certainly have been as viable a proposition for India as miniskirts, had it involved the same amount of financial responsibility as the miniskirt. I am deeply concerned about the financial aspect of the movement. I believe that the economic hazards of an incautious approach are of such magnitude that they can wipe out of existence both FFC and the aspiring film-makers.

Mr. Singh would appear to be quite unconcerned. Perhaps he is in a position to write off people's debts. I am not. I can only point to the pitfalls, having been there before.

LETTER TO NEW STATESMAN

Published in *New Statesman* on 22 March 1974

Sir, John Coleman in his review of my film *Company Limited* (*New Statesman*, 1 March 1974) states that I had worked under Renoir. I wonder where he got this information. It is certainly not in Marie Seton's book about me which Mr Coleman also reviewed in your columns some time ago.

The fact is, when Renoir made *The River* in Calcutta, I had a full-time advertising job. All I was able to do was watch him shooting on a couple of occasions and have some illuminating talks with him in his hotel room.

A second lapse of Mr Coleman's concerns the film itself. The comment on Tagore and the Nobel prize is not made in English but in Bengali, and not by the hero but by his sister-in-law.

WORKING WITH BALA

Published in *National Centre for Performing Arts Journal*, Bombay, December 1976

A tall girl with long limbs and a round face doing a kind of dance I had never seen before against a giant sounding board that was a feature of the now-vanished Senate Hall in Calcutta. The year was 1935, and the occasion was the All-Bengal Music Conference. I remember the applause that greeted Balasaraswati's first performance, and the first performance ever of Bharatnatyam, in Calcutta. I was a schoolboy then, growing up in my maternal uncle's house in South Calcutta. A friend of the family was the impresario Haren Ghosh. Three or four years ago, Harendra had taken us to see Uday Shankar making his debut in Calcutta. It was Harendra again who told us about Bharatnatyam, and the young South Indian dancer who was supposed to excel in it. Since we trusted Harendra's judgement in these matters, we all went to see Balasaraswati.

It didn't take long after her Calcutta performance for Bala to turn into a legendary figure in Indian classical dancing. When in 1966 my friend Dr Narayana Menon asked me to make a short film on Balasaraswati, I was delighted to accept the offer. Although I didn't fancy myself as a maker of documentaries, I felt that a film which would preserve the art of someone who was supreme in her field was worth making. I must say I felt a keen disappointment when negotiations broke down and the film had to be shelved. Judging by her performance in Calcutta at that time, Bala had seemed to be at the top of her form, and the one talk I had with her had suggested that she was eager that the film should be made.

Candid interactions in between the shoot of *Bala* at Marina Beach, Chennai. Photograph by Sandip Ray

What transpired to upset our plans I never found out. I accepted it philosophically as one of the many disappointments a film maker has to face in his career, little knowing that exactly ten years later the offer would come back to me, and from the same source, and that I would find myself in Madras with my crew, all set to film my half-hour homage to Bala.

As we drove to Bala's house on the morning after our arrival, I felt a twinge of regret at having missed her in her prime. I consoled myself with the thought that Bala filmed at fifty-eight was better than Bala not being filmed at all.

The regal presence that confronted us as we crossed the threshold of her house took my breath away. Bala had lost weight — due to diabetes, I'd been told — but had lost none of her poise and vitality. Face to face with her, I felt a fresh surge of enthusiasm for the film.

We sat in the light and airy drawing room, with Bala's illustrious ancestors looking down at us from the walls, drank coffee and talked about the film. Bala could follow English

The shoot of *Bala* in progress. Photograph by Sandip Ray

but wouldn't speak it, so we spoke to her through her daughter Lakshmi. While she talked, or even while she listened or sat idle, I noticed that Bala kept flexing the long tapering fingers of her hands almost incessantly. It seemed as if the playful and restless fingers were an indication that she was perpetually poised on the edge of dancing.

I told Bala that the early part of the film would attempt to trace her career with the help of photographs, newspaper clippings and the like. In a matter of minutes, Lakshmi had brought out and dumped before us scores of scrapbooks and photo albums. It took us hours of poring over them to decide what we would need for our film.

I also wished to include a few glimpses of Bala at home. How did she spend her day, I asked her. Well, it turned out that she spent a lot of time in her garden among her flowers, and an almost equal amount of time in the kitchen cooking (we had a chance to find out how good she was at it). She also did her puja regularly, gave Lakshmi daily dancing lessons, played her favourite game of *pasha* with her and occasionally entertained friends. I asked her if she would let us show in the film some of the things she had just described. "Anything you like," she replied, "except the cooking. I won't have you photograph me in the kitchen!" "What about a family meal with your daughter and your two brothers?" (Ranga and Viswa were home on vacation from the USA where they teach). "That's fine," she said, and her eyes twinkled as Lakshmi translated, "Mother says if you want to be realistic you have to show her phial of insulin right next to her plate."

The high point of my experience was, of course, the shooting of the musical items. We had decided to include two: a *padam* to display her mime and her singing and a *varnam* to reveal the full range of her dancing. For the first, we chose the ineffable *Krishna ni Begane Baro* which I had seen her perform forty years ago, and on every subsequent occasion that she appeared in Calcutta. I had planned to shoot it in a seaside location and had found a beautiful, secluded beach about twenty miles from Madras on the way to Mamallapuram. I felt the open-air setting and the natural light would be a nice contrast to the *varnam* which I was going to shoot in artificial light in the studio against a black backdrop.

As we arrived on the beach on the day of the shooting (which happened to be our last day in Madras), I found a fairly strong breeze blowing. I asked Bala with some trepidation if this would interfere with her dancing. "Oh no," she said, "I can manage." And manage she did. I can think of no other dancer who can use her hand so that it serves the needs of *abhinaya* one moment, and comes down in a graceful arc the next to restrain a billowing sari.

It was Bala herself who chose the *varnam* "Mohamana" for her second and final item in the film. I knew Bala could spin out a *varnam* for over an hour and hold a discerning audience spellbound for its whole length. I also knew that she had been rehearsing her piece for the film at home. I asked Lakshmi how long this particular version of the *varnam* would run. She said, "Mother had whittled it down to twelve minutes. She says she can't make it any shorter." I was anxious that the dance should go into a single reel, as otherwise it would involve a changeover in the projection, causing an inevitable jerk in the music. I should have been happier had the dance been a trifle shorter. At one point I even thought of pointing out to Bala that the exigencies of the 78 rpm gramophone record had at one time obliged even our eminent classical musicians to perform three minute *khayals*, complete with *alap*, *vilambit* and *drut*. But in the end I decided to let Bala have her way, only pointing out that since the film in the camera had to be replenished every five minutes, she would have to do her dance in three parts. As it turned out, Bala had already decided to do it piecemeal, and had split it up into a dozen or so units. This was not out of consideration for the camera, but to ensure perfection in her performance. This striving for perfection, as I learned later, was instilled in her early in her career by her mother. "Remember," she had said, "there will always be at least one crazy person in the audience who will know all the time exactly what you are doing."

In filming the *varnam*, I had the extraordinary experience of turning into a bemused spectator, wholly at the mercy of the performer, but happy in the thought that what the camera was recording was Bala at her resplendent best.

MY WAJID ALI IS NOT "EFFETE AND EFFEMINATE!"

Letter published in *The Illustrated Weekly of India*, 31 December 1978

Ray with Amjad Khan. Photograph by Sandip Ray

Rajbans Khanna deplores the fact that I have chosen to depict Wajid Ali Shah as "effete and effeminate", thus more or less upholding the British view, instead of redressing the balance in his favour which he says I might have done had I "read the right documents".

This is so far from the truth that it almost leads me to believe that Rajbans is incapable of reading a film, let alone reading between the lines.

When Rajbans met me in Delhi three years ago, the shooting of *Shatranj Ke Khiladi* was well under way; which means that the research and sifting of evidence were already over and the screenplay prepared. I did mention to Rajbans that I had read a great deal of relevant documents. Rajbans mentions four in his article: Sleeman's *A Journey Through the Kingdom of Oudh*, Malleson's *The Mutiny of the Bengal Army*, Metcalfe's *Native*

Narratives of the Mutiny and Major Bird's *Dacoitee in Excelsis*. Of these four, Sleeman's account was written at the behest of Dalhousie and was deliberately slanted to provide a pretext for the takeover. Both Malleson's and Metcalfe's accounts deal with the Annexation in so far as it contributed to the 1857 revolt, and both condemn the British action. Only Bird's book deals directly with the Annexation. Wholly sympathetic to Wajid, it launches a sustained and thorough-going attack on British policy, backing it up with copious documentary evidence. The tract gains from the fact that Bird was Assistant Resident of Lucknow during Sleeman's tenure. For Rajban's information, Bird's book provided the principal source for my treatment of the historical part of the film.

THE PRINCIPAL SOURCES

The research for the film took nearly a year. While I personally consulted most of the English and Bengali material in the National and Asiatic libraries, my able collaborators culled evidence from Urdu sources... To give Rajbans some idea of the extent of research, here is a list of the principal sources consulted:

1) *Blue Book on Oude*. This is the official British dossier on the Annexation. It contains among other things, a verbatim account of Outram's last interview with Wajid, and describes Wajid's taking off his turban and handing it to Outram as a parting gesture.

2) Abdul Halim Sharar's *Guzeshta Lucknow* (translated into English by E. S. Harcourt and Fakir Hussain as *Lucknow: The Last Phase of an Oriental Culture*). Sharar was born three years after Wajid's deposition. His father had worked in the Secretariat of Wajid's court and joined Wajid in Metiabruz in 1852. Sharar went and joined his father seven years later. Introducing the book, the translator, say: "The work has long been recognized by Indo-Islamic scholars as a primary source of great value, a unique document both alive and authentic in every detail." Sharar provided most of the socio-cultural details, as well as a fairly extended portrait of Wajid both in his Lucknow and his Metiabruz periods.

3) The Indian histories of Mill and Beveridge, both critical of the Annexation.

4) Two histories of the Mutiny (by Ball and by Kaye).

5) The Letters of Lord Dalhousie. One of these letters provided the information that Outram grumbled about the new treaty and apprehended that Wajid would refuse to sign it. Dalhousie ascribes this attitude to indigestion.

6) *The Reminiscences of Sir Alexander Fayrer.* Fayrer was the Resident Surgeon, Honorary Assistant Resident and Postmaster of Lucknow at the time of his takeover.

7) Two biographies of Outram (by Trotter and by Goldsmith).

8) The diaries and letters of Emily Eden, Fanny Eden, Bishop Heber and Fanny Parkes.

"A MAGNIFICIENT PEOPLE"

Heber visited Lucknow in 1824 when Ghazi-ud-Deen was on the throne. He says: "We had heard much of the misgoverned and desolate state of the Kingdom of Oudh; its peasants, being a martial race, were all armed, but we found them placeable and courteous." No violence and oppression has ever been assigned to him or supposed to have been perpetrated with his knowledge … he urges that all his difficulties have arisen in his entire confidence in the friendship of the Company; that they induced him and his ancestors to disband an excellent army till they scarcely left any sentries for the Palace.

Emily and Fanny were sisters of Lord Auckland. They both visited Lucknow in 1837 during the reign of Muhammad Ali Shah. Fanny records her impression thus: "These people must have been so very magnificent before we Europeans came here with our money-making ways. We have made it impossible for them to do more, and have let all they accomplished go to ruin."

9) *The Indian Mutiny Diary* by Howard Russell. Russell came to India as the correspondent of *The Times.* He was on the spot when the British troops ransacked the Kaiserbagh Palace. He gives the only detailed description of the interior of the palace that I have come across.

10) The young Wajid's personal diary *Mahal Khana Shahi.* This turned out to be an unending account of his armours.

11) The text of Wajid Ali Shah's *Rahas.*

12) Mrs. Meer Hasan Ali's *On the Mussalmans of India* (1832). This was found useful for its details of life in the zanana.

13) *Umrao Jan Ada* (translated into English as *A Courtesan of Lucknow*). This gives a fascinating and authentic picture of Lucknow in Wajid's time.

14) All English and Bengali newspapers and journals of the period preserved in the National Library.

A VOLUPTUARY AND A PUPPET

It was interesting to discover that not all Indian commentators on the Annexation truckled to the British, as Rajbans seems to think, in their estimation of Wajid and the conditions then prevailing in Oudh. One of the most famous Indian journalists of the period, Girish Chunder Ghose, wrote in his weekly, *Hindu Patriot*, a few days before the Annexation: "If Oude is misgoverned, if the King of Oude is a voluptuary and a puppet, if the Minister is a harpy, if the zamindars of Oude are graceless malcontents, we ask, where are the proofs of this lamentable state of things? If a tithe of what is written and said about Oude and its government were true of that country and its governors then society could not have existed there for a day … and a revolution more terrible than the French Revolution would have, despite the presence of the British troops, marked the progress of events in that country."

In addition to all the above, thorough research was done in the Lucknow Musuem, the Victoria Memorial in Calcutta and, later in the India Office Library in London. Besides, I was in close touch throughout with Professor Kaukabh of Aligarh University. Prof. Kaukabh happens to be a great grandson of Wajid Ali Shah and is considered to be one of the best authorities in India on Wajid. He has long been working on a book which sets out to be a portrait of Wajid as he really was and not as the British painted him.

What emerged from all this research is there in the film, which is not a full-fledged biography of Wajid, as Rajbans seems to assume, but an attempt at juxtaposing a story (based on Premchand) about two chess-playing jagirdars in Wajid's Lucknow, with the historical event of the Annexation where the protagonists are Wajid and Outram.

The film begins with a seven-minute prologue which attempts to telescope 100 years of Oudh–British relationship. According to all the available evidence, this was marked throughout, right from Shuja down to Wajid, by an anxiety on the part of Nawabs to maintain friendly relations with the Company, in spite of the fact that treaty after treaty progressively stripped them of their territory and their autonomy. (This can be construed as magnanimity or servility or a mixture of both, depending on one's viewpoint.) After the prologue, story and history unfold by turns over a period of one week ending in the day of Annexation. It is necessary to consider whether in the process of juxtaposition Wajid has been shown as the "effete and the effeminate", and no light has been thrown on "the conflicts and contradictions of his many-faceted personality".

In the prologue, Wajid appears in four successive shots. In the first, he plays Lord Krishna in the "raas"; in the second, he leads a Mohurram procession; in the third, he is shown in his harem with half a dozen concubines. The fourth shot shows Wajid at a durbar. The commentary here says that although Wajid did not like much to rule, he was proud enough of his crown to send it be displayed in the Crystal Palace Exhibition (this is borne out of Dalhousie's letter quoted in the film). About Wajid's disinclination to rule, this is what Sharar has to say:

"The first part of Wajid's reign was characterized by the dashing young King paying more than usual attention to the dispensation of justice and army reform … in less than a year he had become tired of this and the old tastes which he had had as heir apparent returned. He started to consort more frequently with beautiful and dissolute women and soon dancers and singers became pillars of the state and favourites of the realm."

In the second scene in which Wajid appears, he is shown at a kathak recital, at the end of which he learns from the Prime Minister Ali Naqi of the fate that awaits him. He upbraids Ali Naqi for his unmanly display of emotion, saying that only poetry and music should bring tears to a man's eyes.

A CONTRADICTORY CHARACTER

In the third long scene, Wajid is fully aware of the sword of Damocles that hangs over him. This is virtually a scene of monologue where Wajid passes through a wide range of moods. He is remorseful one moment, resigned the next, and seething with righteous indignation as the scene ends:

1) Wajid blames his friends who held key positions in the administration for neglecting the affairs of state and reprimands Ali Naqi for accepting a document which he feels should have been thrown in the face of the Resident.

2) Wajid admits that he was unprepared for the kingship, as he was not directly in the line of accession. Nevertheless, he took his duties seriously in the beginning, reforming the army, holding daily parades, etc. But, bound as he was by the Treaty of 1837, he had to forgo them upon orders from the Resident.

3) Frustrated, Wajid turned to poetry and music for solace.

4) "The common people sing my songs", said Wajid, "and they love my poetry because of its candour." (About Wajid's poetry of this period, Sharar says, "Wajid versified his love affairs and hundreds of the amorous escapades of his early youth. He made them public throughout the country and became to a conventional, moral world a self-confessed sinner.")

5) "My people", says Wajid, "who are supposedly ill governed and underfed are the bravest in battle. The British are aware of this, and that is why they are sending troops."

6) If the people are unhappy under his rule, Wajid argues, why don't they cross over to British territory.

7) Convinced by now that he was being wronged, Wajid strides over to the throne, mounts it and declares that if the British wanted his throne, they would have to fight for it.

The scene that follows shows that Wajid has undergone a change of heart. The implication is that he has realized that the Company has the upper hand, and all he can hope for now is moral victory. In spite of been told by the Dewan that the zamindars have offered to help with men and ammunition should the need for resistance arise, Wajid instructs Ali Naqi to disarm the soldiers, dismantle the guns and issue a proclamation to the effect that the people are not to offer any resistance to the British when they march into Lucknow. Prem Chand calls this an act of cowardice and a symptom of decadence.

On the other hand, Major Bird says: "The resolution was all the more laudable since it was well known to him that all Hindus and Moslems in his service had bound

Poster of *Shatranj ke Khiladi* designed by Ray

themselves by the most solemn oaths to die sword in hand in defence of the Sovereign and their country, and the British Sepoys who for the most part came from the Oude frontier would have refused to fire a single shot upon their fathers, brothers, and other relatives."

In the last scene, where Outram presents his ultimatum to the king. Wajid's behaviour departs from the account in the *Blue Book*, as well as from Sharar. Sharar says: "The King, weeping and wailing, made every effort to exonerate himself." I leave it to Rajbans to decide what the omission of this detail has done to my portrait of Wajid Ali.

A MAN OF MANY MOODS

Apart from these five scenes, there are references to Wajid strewn throughout the film. In the first scene following the prologue, Outram, saddled with the task of deposing the king and uneasy at the thought of having to force an illegal treaty on him, is anxious to convince himself that the king is indeed as bad as Sleeman had portrayed him. He questions Weston, his ADC, and is rattled to discover that Weston has succeeded in crossing the cultural barrier and is sympathetic to Wajid's music and poetry. He snubs Weston and hints at his promotion if he would stop prevaricating.

The second scene introduces a Hindu character, Munshi Nandlal, who is not in Prem Chand's story. One of the purposes of this was to establish the important historical fact that friendly relations existed between the two religious groups in Oudh in Wajid's time. Nandlal feels for Wajid and is genuinely concerned about the possibility of drastic action by the Company. Meer and Mirza do not take him seriously.

In the scene between Outram and Fayrer, Outram admits the contradictions in Wajid's character (devout man, doesn't drink, sings, dances, versifies, etc.), which is why he cannot predict the outcome of the proposed interview.

In the scene of Outram's interview with the Queen Mother, Aulea Begum refuses to intercede for Outram to get her son to sign the treaty. "My son has never acted against the Company's interests," she says.

Where, in all this, is the effeminacy? And is this Wajid not complex, enough, contradictor enough? Characterwise, what more could one have done in a full-fledged biography?

Rajbans seems to be hung up on the Mutiny, which could have had no place in *Shatranj Ke Khiladi*. The Mutiny was not sparked off by the Annexation, but by the Enfield rifle rubbing both Hindus and Moslems up the wrong way. The stored up discontent resulting from the Annexation provided fuel at a later stage. No! *Shatranj Ke Khiladi* is not about Wajid, nor is it aimed to build up a case for the Mutiny. Although it does invest the peasant boy Kalloo with a streak of patriotism when the British march into Lucknow. The crux of the theme is to be found at the end of the film, in Meer and Mirza's continuing to play chess in the British way after they have cleared their conscience by admitting that they have been cowardly in their behaviour.

To spell it out for Rajbans, what it says in effect is (a) that Nawabi did not end with the takeover; (b) that upper-class values were only superficially affected by British rule, and (c) that feudal decadence was a contributing factor in the consolidation of British rule in India.

THOUGHTS ON CHILDREN'S FILMS

Published in *Patha Bhavan School Foundation Day Brochure*, 28 June 1981

I f my memory serves me right, the first film I ever saw was *The Thief of Baghdad*, of Fairbanks, the hero. I remember the glistening earrings and the flashing smile, and great leaps from high parapets which made us alternately hold our breath and gasp in astonishment. And, of course, I remember the flying carpet and the winged horse.

I was about five or six at that time. Going to the cinema in those days was like going to the circus, a great occasion, and happened nearly as infrequently. There were fewer cinemas, and fewer films that parents would take their children to. Cartoons were just emerging with Felix the Cat making occasional brief forays, and Mickey Mouse yet to be born. But Chaplin, Buster Keaton and Harold Lloyd were already on the rampage, and delighting millions. What made them so attractive to children was that they were, above all, great clowns and great acrobats. Which child has ever resisted the circus?

In those days, children's films had not yet been categorized. But parents felt safe with the slapstick comedies or with Fairbanks. They knew they would be zestful and they would be clean. Indeed, they were healthy films which cast a glow which stayed for days.

I was too young to see the first *Tarzan*, which was a silent, but saw the second one — *Tarzan the Apeman*, which came on in the early days of sound. Again the irresistible element of the circus was there. Tarzan was a super-acrobat who swung from tree-branch to tree-branch with the ease of a great trapeze artist. And, of course, the animals were there. The trained chimp who was almost a clown, and there was the menace of wild beasts lurking behind bushes which the godlike apeman had to contend with.

In essence, Tarzan up against a horde of wild elephants is the same thing as Chaplin confronted with a squad of Keystone Cops or Fairbanks battling his way through the villainous Pasha's henchmen, or Keaton as a dud soldier changing the course of the Civil War. In each case we recognize the superhero performing super-deeds in the face of overwhelming odds. This has served as the staple of children's stories throughout the ages. With sound came, inevitably, a setback. Spoken words as such have little place in a children's story. In all *Arabian Nights* what speech do we remember except "Open Sesame?" And what, apart from the story-line, do we remember from our own fairy tales, or for that matter, from the Grimms or Anderson? The jingles, of course.

Most children's films in the early days of sound were fatally fettered to speech. The clowns and mimes had no place in this world of spoken words. Keaton and Lloyd disintegrated. Tarzan had to brush up his accent, Chaplin took to talking with the result that Verdoux and Calvero had to inhabit the world of adults.

It was left to Walt Disney to pull the children's film back out of doldrums. In a cartoon, the limit of achievement is marked by the limit of the creator's imagination. Here Disney was richly endowed. At his best — as in *Pinocchio* — he was outstandingly good. One got delighted in gorging oneself with the richness and profusion of his fare.

It is sad but true that one can count on one's fingers the number of sound films which appeal to the child's mind to the same as the best Disney. The Czechs seem to have a flair. They have made splendid puppet films — a genre which has somewhat less freedom than the cartoon. The Russians have done puppets too. One specially remembers Oubratsov's *The Land of Toys*. Among live action films I recall an enchanting Soviet fable called *The Magic Fish*. The only fairy tale which has achieved true flights of fancy is the French *Beauty and the Beast* made by Jean Cocteau.

The fact is that a children's film which has all the qualities of simplicity, spontaneity and universality is perhaps the hardest kind of film to make. This is not surprising, since literature too shows the same kind of dearth. It is indeed a rare gift to be able to feel with the heart of a child while creating with the mind of an adult.

SERGEI EISENSTEIN AND HIS FILMS

Published in the *Eisenstein Cine Club Brochure*, 1983

With *Strike* Eisenstein revolutionized the Soviet cinema. The absence of a so-called plot or story or a central character was unheard of at that time. A pre-Revolution strike was the theme of *Strike* — how the strike begins and

A still from *Strike*

how it is crushed by the employers by the use of force on workers. Working on this simple scheme, Eisenstein imparted great dramatic force to the film. In his choice of types, mis-en-scene and details and by his editing and composition. The editing style he created, he called the Montage of Attractions. As he conceived it, every shot in the film should go on holding, surprising and moving the mind of the auditor by itself or in conjunction with the shots preceding or following.

A comparison of *Mother* and *Potemkin* reveals the differences between the attitudes of two great directors. A geometric design is obvious in Eisenstein's technique. It affects to a certain extent the human aspect of the subject but the central thesis emerges clearly, boldly and sharply. Humanism and lyricism are the properties obvious in Pudovkin's films. He is the master of technique, but he doesn't have the ruthless geometric inevitability

Portrait of Eisenstein by Ray

of Eisenstein. To draw an analogy from music, Eisenstein reminds one of Bach, while Pudovkin is closer to Beethoven. When we had the fortune to see the second part of *Ivan* we realized that if any film deserved to be classed with Shakespeare's work, it would be Eisenstein's incomplete life of Ivan in two parts. Irrelevant controversies have waged around the film on issues like whether the director has betrayed his medium by modelling it on the opera, or whether a film-maker has the right to distort history. But a great work of art stands always beyond criticism.

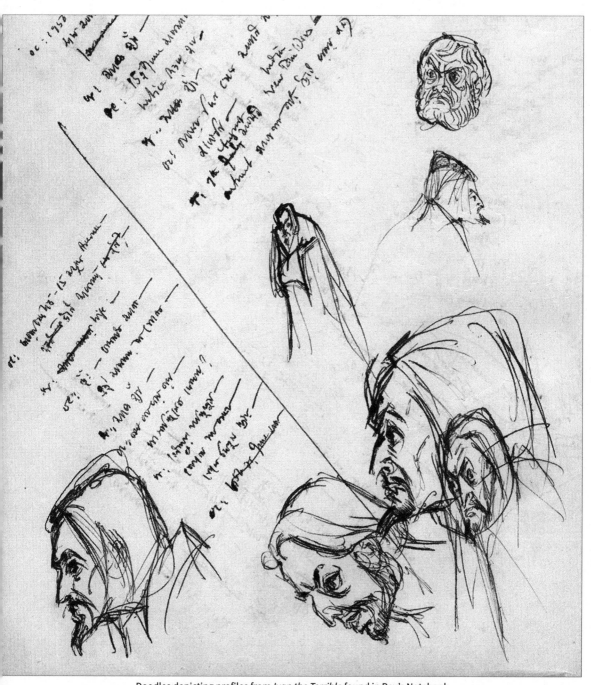

Doodles depicting profiles from *Ivan the Terrible* found in Ray's Notebook

Russian poster of *Battleship Potemkin*

POTEMKIN

Published in the *Eisenstein Cine Club Brochure*, 1987

Our first viewing of *Potemkin* at the Calcutta Film Society was a memorable occasion. This was in the earliest stages of our enthusiasm. We had then only about a dozen members or so. We obtained the print — a 16 mm one — from the British Film Institute at no cost at all. Which means that we were supposed to pay later, but didn't. To this day, we owe the BFI the cost for one copy of *Potemkin*.

We had no theatre to play the print. Eventually, we settled on an empty garage. In due time, in an atmosphere charged with breathless expectation, the film unfolded.

Of course, we were not disappointed. The Odessa steps sequence fully lived up to its reputation. But what surprised me were the other treasures in the film which film books often neglected to describe. The death of Vakulinchuk — the slow, elegiac movement which follows the fireworks of the Odessa steps — is itself a passage of great beauty, deeply affecting and human.

Since then we have seen *Potemkin* at least a dozen times, including an occasion when I ran the film along with a symphony by Sibelius, carefully placing the music so that it echoed the mood of the film. It was an occasion that I was proud of because the experiment worked.

Potemkin is a film that demands to be seen once every two or three years — just as a reminder of what heights the cinema could ride to in those early days.

LETTER TO CINEMA IN INDIA

Published in *Cinema in India*, July–September 1987

Chidananda Das Gupta, in his article "TV Was Born to Talk?" in the April Issue of your magazine, suggests that there is a basic difference between cinema and TV, and that the cinematic approach, when applied to television, does not work. While it is true that TV can bear the weight of words better than cinema, that long shots often lose their impact on the small screen, and that TV requires more frequent use of close-ups, the fact remains that some of the most lauded films on TV — such as the superb Sherlock Holmes series, *Jewel in the Crown*, the films from the Trollope novels — use a technique which is indistinguishable from cinema. Therefore, to say "to try to put cinema on television" has no meaning. Besides, in a few years time there will be devices to blow up considerably the TV image, thus wiping out any difference that may exist between cinema and television.

RESPONSE TO THE 1967 RAMON MAGSAYSAY AWARD

Transcript of the address published in *Bibhab Special* winter issue, 2000

I n my country, in the days of my boyhood, the cinema was apt to be looked upon by the elderly and the conservative with a certain distaste. This applied more to the profession than to the films themselves. One could enjoy going to the movies, but that didn't necessarily imply that one would approve of a member of one's family joining the film profession.

When I decided, some fifteen years ago, to plunge into this very profession, such prejudices were already on the way out, but I made at least one person unhappy and that was my mother.

When my first film won a festival prize, my mother was pleasantly surprised. From that time onwards, until her death some years ago, she grew to be proud of my work, and of the prizes which came to me from all parts of the world.

For myself, I have never ceased to be surprised at the fact that my films have been able to reach audiences beyond the limits of my own country. I am surprised because my films are stories about people who form a tiny segment, not only of humanity as a whole, but of India itself.

I feel particularly honoured and gratified by the Magsaysay Award because it relates not only to the craftsmanship of my films, but to their content as well. Unlike some other arts such as music and painting, cinema, by its very nature, makes concrete statements about people and society. If through my films I have been able to make statements which have been found illuminating, and therefore worthy of recognition, and if through them I have been able to convey some of the joys and sorrows of my people, as well as some of the unique flavour of my country, I would feel more than compensated for my efforts, and more than hopeful about the work that lies ahead.

Once again, may I express my sincere gratitude to the Magsaysay Award Foundation for the great honour they have bestowed on me.

The Certificate of the 1967 Ramon Magsaysay Award

Ray during the shooting of *Seemabaddha*, 1971. Photograph by Sandip Ray

Ray during the shooting of *Sadgati* at Mahasamund (Chattisgarh), 1980. Photograph by Sandip Ray

PERSONAL NOTES

Portrait of Upendrakishore drawn by Ray

UPENDRAKISHORE

A brief note on his grandfather Upendrakishore Ray. Previously unpublished, c. 1963

U. Ray was born in 1862* and died in 1915.

He was writer, painter, musician and scientist — and made outstanding contributions in each capacity.

He was a pioneer of children's literature in Bengal. The children's magazine *Sandesh* which he founded in 1913 set an incredibly high standard in form and content. He wrote illustrated version of *Ramayana* and *Mahabharata* for children which Tagore thought unsurpassable. He also wrote tender versions of Bengali folk tales, and a fascinating series of accounts of prehistoric animal life.

As a musician, he composed many wonderful children's songs and Brahmo Samaj hymns which are still regularly sung. He also wrote text books on the playing of various musical instruments which were models of their kind.

As a scientist, his main contribution — revolutionary even by Western reckoning — were in the field of printing and block making. In fact, he was the first to introduce half tone blocks into India, and in time, incorporate improvements in its methods which were adopted in Western countries. This is particularly astonishing in view of the fact that he never had a chance to go abroad, and was completely self-taught.

* U. Ray was born in 1863. Ray erroneously mentions it as 1862

Satyajit Ray

3 Lake Temple Road, Calcutta 29   *Phone 46-1817*

Upendrakishore Ray

U. Ray was born in 1862 and died in 1915.

He was writer, painter, musician and scientist – and made outstanding contributions in each capacity.

He was a pioneer of children's literature in Bengal. The children's magazine SANDESH which he founded in 1913 set an incredibly high standard in form and content. He wrote illustrated versions of Ramayana & Mahabharata for children which Tagore thought unsurpassable. He also wrote tender versions of Bengali folk tales, & a fascinating series of accounts of prehistoric animal life.

As a musician, he composed many wonderful children's songs and Brahmo Samaj hymns which are still regularly sung. He also wrote text books on the playing of various musical instruments which were models of their kind.

P.T.O

Facsimile of the article written on his letterhead (front page)

As a scientist, his ~~many~~ main contribution — revolutionary even by Western reckoning — were in the ~~xxxx~~ field of printing and blockmaking. In fact, he was the first to introduce half tone blocks into India, and ~~xxx~~, in time, incorporated improvements in its methods which were adopted in Western countries. This is particularly astonishing in view of the fact that he never had a chance to go abroad, and was completely self-taught.

Facsimile of the article written on his letterhead (back page)

SF

Published in *Now*, 21 October 1966

Kuladaranjan Ray's translation of *Mysterious Island*, cover designed by Ray

Heaven knows the initials are not as widely familiar as one would wish. But to the true aficionado, that sibilant and that fricative are the hiss and swish of the rocket that takes him to the farthest reaches of man's fancy, into the blackness of outer void, beyond the galaxies and beyond solar systems yet to be perceived and christened.

In his survey of science fiction, *New Maps of Hell*, Kingsley Amis observes that addiction to the genre occurs either at adolescence or not at all. I have a feeling he is right, because I am yet to meet an adult addict who didn't say he had "been reading the stuff for a very long time".

In my own case, it happened around the age of ten, when my granduncle Kuladaranjan Ray's splendid translation of Jules Verne's *Mysterious Island* came out in two yellow volumes. I was enthralled then as I am now by Verne's power to grip and persuade by sheer abundance of convincing detail. Verne was, of course, the pioneer, but not the sort of pioneer that makes tentative advances into a new territory and leaves it to posterity to do the exploring. He was prodigiously gifted with a speculative imagination. On the top of that he was both industrious and thorough. He wrote his first fantasy *Five Weeks in a Balloon* at the age of thirty-five. From then on he produced one or two such novels every year for something like thirty years. And in all these years, while there were indifferent works interspersed between striking and important ones, Verne never repeated himself thematically.

Verne realized early the pitfalls of the new genre; for instance, you couldn't afford to let the fantasy soar, like a fairy tale, on a plane of pure make-believe. It had to have trappings of reality, and all the manner of pains had to be taken so that the reality didn't find itself adrift in a sea of speculation. One of the devices Verne used was to take the characters part of a carefully recreated historical event into the fabric of the fantasy. Thus the American Civil War triggers off an escape in a balloon which lands its occupants in the mysterious island. The Sepoy Mutiny and the Nana Sahib are very much part of *Tigers and Traitors*, a fantasy laid in India. *Around the World in Eighty Days*, though not a science fantasy, is nevertheless a pretty tall story which encircles the globe and colours every episode in every country with touches of authentic local details. The episode in India is particularly rich in information on the then newly opened railways.

Verne read H. G. Wells and spoke disparagingly of his improbable flights of fancy. Reading Wells today, one sees the points of Verne's objection. Wells' approach to science fiction was poetic and romantic, and he had all the romantic poetic aversion to cold facts. How does the invisible man become invisible? We don't know because the three fat leather-bound notebooks which hold his secret are with the landlord of "that little inn in Port Stowe", and he will neither part with them nor disclose their contents. This is how Griffin, the Invisible Man himself, describes the process to his physician friend:

"I will tell you Kemp, sooner or later, all the complicated processes. We need not go into that now … but the essential phase was to place the transparent object whose refractive index was to be lowered, between two radiating centres of a sort of ethereal vibration, of which I will tell you more fully later … I wanted two little dynamos, and these I worked with a cheap gas engine. My first experiment was with a wool fabric …"

TIME MACHINE

There are two typical Wells elements in this: a dash of scientific patter, and a modus operandi that is made to sound absurdly simple, and yet is wholly never described. Take *The Time Machine*. Here even the scientific patter has been dispensed with, save for a brief reference by the Time Traveller to the theoretical possibilities of travelling in the 4th Dimension. The machine is thus described:

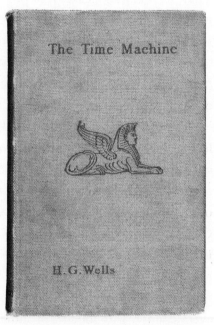

The first UK edition of *Time Machine*, William Heinemann, London, 1895

"The thing that the Time Traveller held in his hand was a glittering metallic framework, scarcely larger than a small clock, and very delicately made. There was ivory in it, and a transparent crystalline substance …"

"This little affair," said the Time Traveller, resting his elbow on the table and pressing the hands together above the apparatus, "is only a model. It is my plan for a machine to travel through time. You will notice that it looks singularly askew, and there is an odd twinkling appearance about this bar, as though it was in some way unreal … also, here is one little white lever, and here is another."

One lever for the past and one for the future — what could be simpler? Although a scientist, Wells chose, in his science fiction, to skirt technology and concentrate on fiction. What really fascinated is not the breakthrough itself, but its aftermath. This gave Wells a freedom and flexibility which Verne never had. Verne devoted twenty-six chapters out of a total of twenty-eight of *From the Earth to the Moon* to describing and making of the projectile that was to make the first lunar trip. Although his mode of moon travel will hardly do for our time, the story at least proves that his main concern was technology. Throughout his career he kept stressing this aspect, prognosticating on its basis and coming up with inventions that confront man with new sensations, new experiences, new adventures. If his science now appears perfunctory, his prescience does not, for he was able to foresee, among other things, the submarine, the helicopter, television, motion picture and space flight.

Today we grant both Verne and Wells honourable places in hierarchy of science-fiction writers. Apart from being pioneers, they are the progenitors of the two main types of science fiction as it exists today. We may roughly term them as prosaic and poetic. The first uses available scientific data as a springboard, but never lets the imagination soar beyond the limits of probability. The second gives freer rein to fancy, either ignores or circumvents facts, and tries to build conviction on a poetic plane. Of course, there are numerous stories where these two overlap, and some of the best modern science fiction is being written by scientists like Arthur Clarke and Isaac Asimov who achieve fine prophetic plights of fancy without losing their grip on scientific postulates.

In this era of rapidly developing technology, science fiction is inevitably undergoing transformations. The old staples are being replaced by new ones, and the field is being constantly enriched by new breakthroughs in every branch of applied science. The laser beam, computer machines, space satellites, Androids (which are robots in human forms), suspended animation — these are among common ingredients of contemporary science fiction. The moon is now nearly out as a field of speculation. Invisibility and Time Travel have been proved scientifically unattainable, and have lost their status as staples. Robots are having a field day, but malevolent ones are frowned upon, as hostility is regarded as a psychological state which a machine is incapable of attaining. ESP or Extra-Sensory Perception is coming into its own, thanks to recent findings, and extraterrestrials are being freely endowed with the powers of hypnosis and telepathy.

For the poets, the most fertile field would to be the extraterrestrial, to which lack of knowledge imparts the nebulousness necessary for the poetic imagination to work upon. Even Mars, the nearest planet, remains clouded, both literally and metaphorically. But of course, the SF writer hardly restricts himself to our solar system. The field today is virtually limitless.

But any story of human endeavour on a familiar terrestrial plane has to have the backing of scientific data. Rockets may soar out into space but if they set out from the earth, and if they contain human beings, there is no other way to but treat the happenings in a factual, scientific way.

But this is not necessarily an inhibiting factor. For one thing, the imponderables of human behaviour are always there to set off against the cold predictability (barring accidents) of machines. For another, for the vast mass of lay readers, technology still has enough elements of fantasy in it. As long as a man himself has not sensed weightlessness, or felt the sheering upthrust of the rocket or fathomed a fraction of the infinite complexities of a giant computer, for him the elements of wonder will persist in clinging to the very ideas.

It is this sense of wonder that science fiction thrives on, and will continue to do so as long as there are men willing to dip into a tale that will make him feel small in the face of an expanding universe, and let him share the triumph and the futility of men probing into spheres of darkness — in space, on earth, in an alien planet, or in his own mind and body.

BGHS

Published in *Ballygunge High School Alumni Association 'Praktoni Sangha' Brochure*, 1967

The more one gets on in years, the happier one's memories of schooldays seem to be. My own recollections of BGHS are still green enough to be recalled in all their minutiae, and I am sure this applies to many others of my time, or even earlier. Of course there were a few unsavory episodes — such as the Drill Master (whose shirt collars were so expansive, they flapped in the breeze like pigeon's wings) barking out at me to execute a high jump clearly beyond my capacity — but they do nothing to dim the glow that pervades these memories.

We made special efforts, I remember, to reach school at least half an hour before classes started. We used this extra time to sharpen our skill at marbles or top-spinning. There was a time when the yo-yo came suddenly into vogue, and hands went bobbing up and down, even surreptitiously, in the class, in an effort to master a new and difficult art. But the vogue was a short-lived one, and, at any rate, never quite replaced the marble and top.

The classes themselves never fell into monotony, largely because of the unconscious entertainment provided by a great variety of masters. As I think back on them, each one seems to have been unique in his own way. There was M--, with his frequent lapses into profound absent mindedness ("May I go out, sir?" "Very good"); there was B--, Sanskrit Master, as well as master of the hyperbolic reprimand ("Can't you see I've been shouting so much that blood has been gushing out of my mouth?"). There was G-- who taught Bengali, who was time and again made to recall the touching episode in his life that had brought

Ray's sketch of Ballygunge Government High School

forth a certain poem of his which we had to study; there was A--, whose knowledge of English didn't measure up to the knowledge of the craft he taught, so that whenever the durwan brought in a notice to be read out to the class, he would pretend to be busy and get one of the boys to perform the task. B--, who taught English grammar, had to serve for a long time on the jury in a famous murder trial, and was obliged, throughout this period, to intersperse his lessons in the class with accounts of the latest sensational exposures.

At tiffin time we bought a pice-worth of *Alur dom* in a sal-leaf container and stabbed the potato with a stick to convey it to our mouth. "Happy Boy" — the prototype of latest brands of ice-cream such as Magnolia and Kwality — made its appearance in our time. Wrapped in translucent paper like butter, it soon invaded the precincts of our school and caused much anxiety to contending caterers.

We looked forward to the summer when classes were held in the morning. The sunlight streamed through the windows and struck the walls and the blackboards to light up the classrooms in a strange, unfamiliar way. The classes being shorter, the fun was more concentrated, with a lot of time left after school to romp about in the playground.

The high points of excitement were reached at Saraswati Puja, on the Annual Sports day, and the prize-giving day. These were true 'occasions', when the school was decked out, and the air was filled with a tense exhilaration, and everybody went about feeling important. The prize winners felt proud of themselves, and those who didn't win felt proud of those who did, and of course everybody felt proud of the school.

In my own sense, school period lasted only five years, and yet, it seems like a whole lifetime of memorable experiences, so rich and full are its memories. Is this a case of distance lending enchantment? I don't think so. I think schoolboys have an innate and inexhaustible capacity to impart a leavening of gaiety into what would otherwise be a fairly drab routine of study and exams.

I hope BGHS hasn't changed too drastically over the years. But even if it has, I'm sure schoolboys haven't, and when the boys of today go out, they will carry with them the same sort of enchanted memories as we did, and as every other school boy in every age and clime had done ever since schools came into existence.

FESTIVAL FLASHBACKS

Talk delivered at Max Muller Bhavan, German Cultural Institute, Kolkata, and published in *Amrita Bazar Patrika* Puja Annual, 1967.

There are two possible reasons for an Indian film-maker to be present at an international film festival in Europe. Either he can have a film in competition, in which case he goes as part of the official delegation invited by the festival, usually consisting of the producer of the film, its director, and one or two of its leading players or he can go as a member of the International Jury that decides the date of competing films. I have gone in both capacities.

The first time one of my films was shown in a European festival was in Cannes in 1957. This film was *Pather Panchali*. I didn't go then, because I wasn't invited. But because *Pather Panchali* won a prize, I was invited to Venice the following year. Ever since then, I've been going to festivals with a fair regularity, either as a judge, or as a competitor. Four of my seven films entered so far have won prizes, and with what I like to think of as unerring foresight, the three times that my films didn't get a prize were the three occasions I decided to stay back.

THIRD DEGREE

If I were asked to make a choice between going as a judge and going as a competitor, I would not find it easy. Both experiences have elements of the third degree in them, and both have pleasurable aspects. If you are on the jury, you are obliged to sit through all the competing films. This is not so tough in Venice, where you have fourteen films, and two weeks to

Ray with the Golden Bear at Berlin, 1973

see them in. Moscow in 1963 had forty-four full length features, and Berlin in 1962 had thirty-five, and two weeks is the normal running time for all major festivals. Imagine a situation where you have to spend eight hours a day for 14 days in a darkened theatre, looking at films, most of which are spoken in strange tongues, which you strive to follow through translations conveyed by way of microphones while keeping one ear free for the original soundtrack, because as a judge you must take the vital factor of music into account, and finally take part in learned discussions on their merits as works of art — and you will realize that the festival judge's lot is not an enviable one. The compensations are in the few really good films that turn up from time to time, both from expected and unexpected sources — and in the intellectual exercise one gets from discussing films — good, bad or indifferent — with the directors, critics and actors that normally make up a jury.

If you go as a competitor, you are not obliged to sit through all the films shown. But it's always difficult to decide what to see and what to leave out, because you don't want to miss that dark horse that eventually bags the trophy; with the result that you generally end up by seeing most of the films, at least up to the point where they hold the threat of a possible contender. Even when a film lacks artistic merit, it may have attractions of other sorts. It's a great game in the festivals these days to watch out for the bedroom scene, to find out what it holds in the way of frank exposure. In Berlin two years ago, every film seemed to top the previous one in this respect, until the official Japanese entry three days from the end of the festival finally demolished the last remaining barrier between films for public exhibition, and those for more esoteric and vicarious consumption, known by the same name as one of Picasso's more famous periods.

However, even if going to a festival is not quite one long round of pleasure, there are many aspects to it that are enjoyable, and many experiences that one remembers with pleasure and gratitude.

FIRST BERLIN TRIP

My first trip to Berlin was in 1961. I went to serve on the jury for feature films. Before then, I had served on juries at Brussels and Vienna, but they were not major festivals, and I was looking forward to the Berlin trip. I had learnt about the entries beforehand, and there were important films among them. For instance, the latest works of Antonioni, Jean-Luc Godard and Kurosawa.

As I got out of my plane at the airport, I was met by a smiling middle-aged gentleman who said his name was Herbert Luft, and that he was supposed to look after the members of the jury. One of the first things I asked Mr. Luft was his height. He said he was exactly one metre and ninety-nine centimeters, which made him a good five centimeters taller than I. But Luft's towering physicality was counterbalanced by a persistent geniality, which made it seem as if he were always at the point of apologizing for being in a class by himself, and not being able to do anything about it.

DISCREET NUDGE!

Talking in the car, as we drove from the airport to our destination in the city, I was struck by Luft's deep knowledge and love for cinema. He said he had been doing this job of looking after the jury ever since the inception of the Berlin film festival. He was full of intriguing accounts of the behaviour of judges at past festivals. The famous American

Sidney Poitier, Rod Steiger, Anil Chatterjee and Ray (from left to right) strike up a conversation at Berlin, 1963

comedian Harold Lloyd had been elected president of the previous year's jury. While accepting the nomination, Llyod had confessed that he was a bit out of touch with the movies. His behaviour during the screenings had made it quite clear that he was not too keen to re-establish the contact, and it had fallen upon Luft to give the president a discreet nudge every time he tended to doze off — which happened more and more frequently as the festival progressed.

The members of our jury, however, included no hallowed figures from the past. It consisted of people actively engaged, either in the making of films — producing and directors — or in writing about them — film critics. The latter included one of the oldest and most respected of Japanese critics — Ushihara — who spent a good part of the screening time hunched over his notebook with a flashlight pen in his hand, anxious to preserve immediate reactions at the expense of screen footage. Our American colleague was the director Nicolas Ray, who had started out with great promise as a maker of films of social protest, but had been reduced by circumstances to making yet another widescreen Biblical epic in colour.

PACKED PROGRAMME

We were put up in a small but comfortable hotel — the Park Zellermayer — tucked away in a quiet sidestreet, but still within strolling distance of the festival's offices. In 1961, they were in the Hotel Amzoo in Kurfurstendamm, Berlin's main thoroughfare. The isolation is important for the jury, because festivals make a great point of keeping the jury's deliberations a secret. As I said before, we were to judge thirty-five films in the space of fourteen days. Out of these thirty-five, about twenty-five had to be seen in public showings at the Zoo Palast. This is the 2000-seater cinema which holds the festival screenings. The remaining ones had to be seen in a miniature cinema called the Lilliput. Screening competitive films in the Lilliput yielded an unexpected advantage. The audience here was composed entirely of the members of the jury. If, by the third reel of any film, it was unanimously felt that it didn't show any signs of being a possible contender, we would stop the screening, and give our eyes that little extra rest before we tackled the second feature of the day at three o'clock. This worked beautifully, except in the case of a Korean film, where one member of the jury — the Belgian — kept discovering beauties wholly imperceptible to the other ten.

The second feature at the Zoo Palast ended at about 5.30, and the only time the jury had to themselves was between then and 8 in the evening. The evening performance at 9 was inevitably followed by a midnight party, given by one of the competing countries. The scope of these parties was usually in direct ratio to the financial prosperity of the country concerned. Their usefulness consisted in the opportunities for lobbying they presented. A great deal of buying and selling goes on at these festivals throughout the fortnight. In the year I'm talking about, an American company was responsible for the production of two high-budget films, both shot in Spain. They were *El Cid* and *King of Kings*. The former had Charlton Heston as the leading star, and the latter was being made by our colleague, Nicholas Ray. The official American entry at the festival had something to do with the South Sea Islands. The American party in Berlin was given by the American Motion Picture Export Association in the main dining hall of the Berlin Hilton. This was done up for the occasion in a Hawaiian style, complete with a Hula band and grass-skirted starlets. Posters for *El Cid* and *King of Kings* were strewn about the hall, Heston flew over to make a personal appearance, while Nicholas Ray stopped brooding about competing films, and held forth on the mid-Atlantic accent he had devised for Jesus Christ.

Heston turned out to be a serious student of the cinema. Encounters with stars, however brief, can sometimes be quite revealing. This is because one tends to identify them with the kind of parts they play, wheras, face to face, they often reveal traits which one wouldn't have believed they possessed. I have met a great number of acting celebrities on my five visits to Berlin. I found the young modern actors — such as Poitier, Claire Bloom, Hardy Kruger or Anna Karina — to be quite without affectation. The only actor who seemed determined to live up to his screen image was the German Curt Jurgens.

It must be noted here that Berlin is not like Lido or Cannes, where for the fifteen days of the festival, the whole place puts on a festive garb, as it were. Both Cannes and Lido are small places and even at ordinary times, the Casino and the beach mark them out as playgrounds. In Berlin, the festival makes itself felt over an area of approximately four square miles. This includes the half a dozen or so fine hotels where the delegates stay, most of the restaurants listed on the meal coupons given to the delegates, the handsome new Europa Center where all the official work of the festival is done, and the four or five cinemas where the films in and out of competition play. Of these cinemas, one small one right next to the Zoo Palast is given over to the showing of old classics. On my first trip, as a conscientious member of the jury, I was in despair to catch up with some of the famous old German films. But I made it on my second trip. The screenings were made memorable not only by the films, but by the anonymous pianist, who sat in the dark with his eyes on the screen, and improvised accompaniments to silent films with a style and tact that would be the envy of all professional film composers.

BREATHTAKING

Apart from the screenings and the parties, the official programme of the festival included a star parade in the splendid open-air amphitheatre in the woods, a boat trip down the Spree, a film ball, and a final winding-up party hosted by the director of the festival. The star-parade was notable for the dazzling efficiency of organization, and the splendour of the brass band. There was one enchanted moment when, in the falling light of dusk, just before the floodlights came on, every person in an audience of 25,000 struck a match precisely at the same instant, so that we had a brief but breathtaking spectacle of a sort of Teutonic Dewali on a Wagnerian scale.

ON KU'DAMM

In the little time that one has to oneself in the midst of peremptory engagements, one tends to roam the streets — particularly Kurfurstendamm — where a great deal seems to happen most of the time. It is on Kurfurstendamm — which the Berliners shorten to Ku'damm — that the skeletal remains of the Kaiser Wilhelm Church stand as a reminder of the Second World War. On one side of the ruins is the squat, octagonal defiantly simple and modern memorial church, while on the other side is the high octagonal bell tower that goes with it. The modern structure is designed in harmonious contrast to the ruins, and I for one find it a striking and valid conception, although the Berliner seems sceptical about it. But then, the Berliner seems sceptical about the most modern versions of old landmarks. They refer to the new Congress Hall as the Pregnant Oyster, and I'm sure they have a name for the new opera too, which has a black facade, and black jutting-out balconies that look like wardrobe drawers.

About 200 yards from the church across the street is the Berlin zoo and aquarium. In the gardens of the zoo, on Sunday mornings, one can listen to an excellent concert of light classical music. But for me, the most striking feature of the zoo was the special enclosure for the Indian cow, right next to the African Zebu. If the cow showed any signs of recognition in being confronted by a fellow Indian, I failed to notice it. But it certainly brought home to me more forcibly the fact of being in a foreign country than anyone else I encountered in Berlin.

The pedestrian's progress on the Ku'damm is often slowed down by the presence of the artists. These artists spread themselves over a large area over the pavement and draw with coloured chalk enormous replicas of well known masterpieces. I have found the same artist at work on a single painting from morning till sunset. Most of these pavement painters are art students, while others are struggling professionals who use what collects in their hats to buy paint materials. The artists leave at the end of the day, but their works remain, and it's not unusual, in the evenings, to find oneself stepping over a Mona Lisa, or the Venus by Boticelli, or an abstraction by Braque or Picasso. Also in evidence in the streets are what can be described as the human counterparts of the Kaiser Wilhelm Church: the disabled veterans of the war. The most prominent of these sits in a wheel chair with a full-grown eagle perched on his left hand, with the right hand stretched out, holding a hat.

WORK OF THE JURY

In the films in competition, if there's one that stands out head and shoulders above the others, it makes the work of the jury much simpler. In Brussels, the final meeting of the jury to decide on the winners lasted sixteen hours. In Berlin, it was over in less than an hour. The winner was Antonioni's *La Notte*. Apart from being a just prize, it was a popular one too. A festival audience can be quite openly vocal in commenting on a prize. Sometimes, they are also vocal during a screening, as well as at the end, when the director gets up on the stage and takes his bow in the glare of spotlights. This is the way they do it in Berlin. In Venice, the director doesn't have to leave his seat in the front row of the upstairs balcony. He has the spotlight turned on him at the end of the performance, and all he does is get up and bow, making sure that he leans over enough for the people downstairs to see who they're cheering, or booing, as the case may be. I have seen a director from Argentina, whose film had been hissed at all the way through, stand up at the end of the show and take a bow and receive a fresh barrage of catcalls lasting a full minute, in the relentless glare of spotlights. I don't know if this director is still in business, but I can think of milder

John Boorman, Billy Wilder, Michelangelo Antonioni and Ray (from left to right) at the Cannes Film Festival, 1982

traumatic experiences crippling an artist for good.

Next to Moscow, Berlin has probably the most patient and polite audience in the world. In fact, they are so polite that the maker of an unfortunate Turkish film once mistook a good humoured castigation for whole-hearted approval, and made a protracted show of buoyant gratitude, until a single, full-throated boo from the back of the auditorium hastened him off the stage.

GLOBAL FRATERNITY

I have been lucky so far in the reception to my films. I haven't won a Golden Bear yet, but since the gold prize goes to the financier, and since I never finance my own films,

I'm happier to get the silver prize. Having gone three times with competing films, I have managed to get rid of my tension and can afford to skip some of the screenings, and use the time to chat with visiting film-makers who come from other parts of the world. It's surprising how quickly and how well a film-maker gets along with other film-makers. They seem to belong to a global fraternity which speaks the same language, think the same thoughts and faces the same problems. Last year in Berlin I met the Polish Roman Polanski, the American Dick Lester, who made those Beatles films, and the young German director Schloendorf. The West Germans are not proud of their own product, and with good reason. But Schloendorf seems to have the guts and the talent to bring about a change, and he seemed bent upon doing so. Of course, we had a great deal to talk about — about new equipment, and what they're doing to expand the language of the cinema, and about the all-important universal problem of how to cut down on cost without cutting down on quality.

WITH CRITICS

With critics you feel less at ease, because they often tend to see more in your work than you do, so that you are faced with the situation where you can set them right only at the risk of reducing your own work in their eyes. The Oriental film-maker is especially prone to overinterpretation by Western critics. By the very nature of the medium, the language of the cinema has a twofold aspect to it. One relates to the surface and is therefore readily available to everybody, while the other has to do with traditional roots. This is what gives the work of an artist the validity that goes with being true to one's own culture. For a foreigner to appreciate this properly needs time, and effort, and connoisseurship. But for reasons best known to himself, a film critic seldom permits himself to act baffled. To him, no mode is an alien mode. He is always ready with his responses, ready to ascribe influences, ready to read meanings into non-symbols. As an example of the grotesque consequences of this attitude, one may cite the reaction of the avant-garde French critic faced with a typical Bombay product for the first time: he found the musical interruptions closely related to the Brectian device of Alienation.

I feel safer with people who regard films solely as a commodity — namely, the producers. Safer because one faces here a clear-cut situation and a clear-cut response. The bigger the producer, the less likely is he to make any bones about his dogmas. I shall end my account my describing an encounter in Berlin with one such producer; in fact, one of the biggest of them all.

The term "Movie Moghul" was invented in the thirties to describe some half a dozen of the top bosses of Hollywood film industry.

David Selznick, who died three years ago, was one of them, and I met him in Berlin six months before his death.

Some years back, Selznick had set up an annual award for the best foreign film shown in the United States, and I had already won it twice for the first two parts of my trilogy. I had also received a letter from Selznick in Calcutta suggesting that I should make a film for him on an Indian subject, with a suitable part for his wife, Jennifer Jones. I didn't feel attracted to the idea and had written back to say how busy I was with my several projects.

The correspondence had ended there. But two days after my arrival in Berlin with my film *Mahanagar*, I had a call from the Berlin Hilton from Selznick's secretary. The following day I found myself lunching with the Movie Moghul.

For a good half hour, Selznick regaled me with stories of the stars he had helped to nurture.

I learnt, among other things that Selznick had given up Gregory Peck as a hopeless case after his first film, but was forced to keep him on and build him up because of the stupendous quantity of fanmail he received. I also learnt that Ingrid Bergman was prone to falling in love with every director she worked with — with the exception of Alfred Hitchcock.

Halfway through the lunch, Selznick stopped telling stories and came out with the two requests he had to make. One was that I should give his Indian project some more thought, and the other was that I should present the Selznick trophy for the year to Ingmar Bergman at a ceremony which was to be held in Berlin on the next day. Since I was anxious to pull out of the first proposal, I decided to agree to the second one. I had even stronger reasons now to decline to work for him, because *Life Magazine* had recently brought out an alarming account of the memos that Selznick was in the habit of sending his directors. They were brief but peremptory orders which encroached on a director's freedom, and they had already caused John Huston to walk out of *A Farewell to Arms.*

I told Selznick that I knew about his memos.

Although he gave a broad smile and said he wouldn't do with me what he had done with John; I could see that he was a little deflated, and we didn't talk about the project any more.

The awards ceremony was to take place the next evening. When I came back to my hotel from lunch, there was a sealed envelope waiting for me at the reception. I opened it and brought out a small chit. Printed across the top were the words 'Memo from David O Selznick'. Below were short lines of typescript — the text of the speech I was to make at the ceremony, with a request at the bottom to memorize it.

Well, I did make a speech, but not in Mr. Selznick's words, and I think that was what finally put an end to his Indian project.

MY SUNDAY

Published in *Amrita Bazar Patrika*, 6 January 1988

To me the words "My Sunday" are evocative of a whole range of situations. They do not merely embody the relief that comes after six days of work. This is perhaps because in the course of my life, "Sunday" in its specific literal sense has gradually lost its significance. While working, the days often merge together and Sunday in itself does not mean anything. My Sundays, as I see them, are now moments of leisure which come at various times, in various ways.

Perhaps an outline of my working hours will give a better perspective. When there is shooting, that is shooting in the studio, I leave house at 9 a.m. and work till about 6 o' clock when I return home. Following a bit of rest, I prepare myself for the next day's work which facilitates carrying out the shooting smoothly. The pattern changes when shooting gets over and editing commences, which again involves eight to ten hours of work every day. There are two instances when nobody is allowed to enter my room. The first is when am composing — either background music or songs for my films. This also takes place sometime before the Pujas when I write for even 16 hours a day for the Puja numbers of Bengali journals.

Talking about what I call my Sundays, I do turn on the radio fairly often, particularly the BBC Western classical music programmes broadcast from Calcutta 'B' and the Indian National Programme from Delhi (if I know what's on) figure in my list of favourites. Occasionally I listen to music while working on something else. Buying records is another hobby which has persisted for long and I'm always looking for opportunities to play them. Reading is almost second nature to me. I read till late before going to bed.

If there is time on my hands, I often work on my magazine "Sandesh". This being a monthly, illustration takes up considerable time. I try to illustrate the stories of certain authors myself. This also holds for important articles and particularly Puja numbers. I read and edit manuscripts as well whenever possible.

Children have played a significant part right through my films — beginning from *Pather Panchali* continuing into *Debi, Mahanagar, Jalsaghar* (to some extent) and even in some of my more recent films. In real life, it seems there exists an unspoken understanding between children and myself. They mix with me instinctively and willingly. I too unknowingly observe the children who come over to my house a great deal. Perhaps it is a case of enlightenment through feeling.

Having done without a secretary so far, I am obliged to take care of my own correspondence. So my leisure hours may often find me writing letters.

It may sometimes happen that I find I have nothing to do and I feel I must do something. This is what I call one of my Sundays. It was in fact such an instance which prompted me to begin translating Lear's limericks. My Sundays come upon me rather unexpectedly. I recall an incident once when I was returning from London, in view of some mechanical trouble my plane got delayed at Bombay by sixteen hours. The passengers waited in the lounge of "Sun 'n Sand". I did not know any of the people around me and in those sixteen hours I translated four poems of Sukumar Ray's *Abol Tabol*.

Sunday to me is the time when friends drop in, when the entire morning can be devoted to animated talk — when we discuss almost everything under the sun. If on any such occasion I have a bit too much on my hands, I join in the conversation and work at the same time, combining the two functions. Since I enjoy my work it becomes for me a form of recreation as well. So, the quintessence of my Sundays is not leisure alone, but a happy blending of work and rest.

HOME AND THE WORLD

Published in *The Guardian*, 1 August 1991

My first acquaintance with Tagore was through his songs. When I was a very small child, my mother used to put me to sleep by singing Tagore's songs. Some of them became my favourites and I would ask for them by name when I learnt to speak.

As I grew up, I was exposed to his poems and short stories. I wasn't much of a reader of poetry and I didn't learn his poems by heart as some of my friends did. But I thought his short stories were among the finest ever written. Later, I grew to admire him as a painter — untaught, but extraordinarily found and possessed of an instinctive feeling for rhythm and spacing.

I met Tagore in all about a dozen times, usually in the company of my mother. You couldn't just confront him and make conversation. His physical appearance — the flowing hair and beard, the serene yet penetrating gaze, the robe that reached down to the ankles — all inspired awe, and you found yourself tongue-tied or at best in whispers. He had a voice which was both high-pitched and intensely musical, and he spoke chaste Bengali in a very special accent which was widely imitated, as was his unique and beautiful handwriting. He always had a kind word for me as the grandson of one of his friends and contemporaries, and as the son of one of his young admirers who wrote the first article written to introduce Tagore to English readers in a 1912 issue of *Quest* magazine.

Once when I was 8 years old, I went to Santiniketan — Tagore's Abode of Peace —

Draft sketches for the portrait of Tagore made by Ray in his notebook

and taken to see him by my mother. In my pocket was a newly bought autograph album. I stood before his desk, my mother gave me a nudge, and I produced the small album. "Sir, will you write something in it for me, please?" I whispered. "Leave it with me," he said, "and come back tomorrow to collect it."

I did as told, and he handed me back the album, smiled at my mother and said, "Let him grow up a little, and he'll understand what I've written."

As it turned out, it was a short poem which came to be widely published and admired after his death. What it said was this: I have spent a fortune travelling to distant shores and looked at lofty mountains and boundless oceans, and yet I haven't found time to take a few steps from my house to look at a single dewdrop on a single blade of grass.

One of the things which Tagore used to tell my mother every time we met was — "Why don't you send your son to my school?" It was at my mother's behest that I joined the art school in Santiniketan after my graduation from Calcutta. I consider the three years I spent in Santiniketan as the most fruitful of my life. This was not so much because of the proximity of Tagore, who continued to remain unapproachable. It was just that Santiniketan opened my eyes for the first time to the splendours of Indian and Far Eastern art. Until then I was completely under the sway of Western art, music and literature. Santiniketan made me the combined product of East and West that I am. As a film-maker I owe as much to Santiniketan as I do to American and European cinema. And when I made my first film *Pather Panchali* and embellished it with rural details which I was encountering for the first time, Tagore's little poem in my autograph album came back again and again to my mind.

Ray holding a photograph of Tagore taken by Albert Kahn at Paris, 1981.
Photograph courtesy Anne de Henning

Ray during the shooting of *Jana Aranya*, 1975. Photograph by Sandip Ray

REMINISCENCES

Portrait of Nandalal Bose drawn by Ray

REMINISCENCES OF NANDALAL BOSE: MASTER-MASHAI

Published in *Link*, 1 May 1966

My earliest memories of Nandalal Bose go back to Santiniketan in 1924. I had lost my father a year back, and mother had taken me to the peace and quiet of what was then a true Ashram.

We lived in a cottage not far from where the Kalabhavan was in those days, in the second floor of the buildings which is now the library. Mother bought me a little sketchbook in which I was supposed to draw whatever took my fancy, and show it to Nanda Babu. I still have that sketchbook. It contains only one drawing by me — barely recognizable as a flower — and four by Nandalal Babu: a cow, a tiger with spots, a tiger with strips and a bear attacked by bees. The striped tiger had a black tip to its tail, and I had asked him why it was so. "You see," he had said, "it's like this — the tiger was hungry, and went scrounging for food into a kitchen; and while he looked about for something to eat, the end of his tail flopped into the oven."

In July 1940, I joined Kalabhavan as a student of Fine Arts. When I met him, the first words he said were, "I heard you'd grown very tall, so I had a special taktaposh built for you." Mother said to him — somewhat tactlessly I thought — that I didn't have a very high regard for "Oriental Art". She had obviously drawn her conclusion from the colour plates in "Prabas" — the sentimental insipid variations of classical themes which a handful of painters kept churning out month after month. Master-mashai only smiled and said, "We'll have a chance to talk about that one of these days."

Master-mashai's method, as it gradually revealed itself, was not to impose a style, but to begin by going to the very source of all styles, i.e., Nature. I was sketching a buffalo one day. He walked up to me and glanced at my sketchbook. "One outline's all right," he said. "But where's the feel of the bones beneath the skin? Feel the bones with your pencil. Feel the structure that makes the beast stand and sit and walk. The real truth lies beneath the skin."

The most persistent image I have of Master-mashai is not of sitting at his desk and working but out on his rounds, a chaddar wrapped like a pugree around his head, pyjamas at least four inches above the ankle so that the edges didn't — as ours did — have a lining of red dust. I have no memory of him ever flying into a rage. Indifferent student work usually brought forth sly, sarcastic comment. "Your Santhal has spine all right, but your painting hasn't." Thereupon, he would proceed to explain the anatomy of composition.

In 1942, barely halfway through the course, I left Kalabhavan to take up advertising work in Calcutta. I didn't entirely lose touch with Master-mashai, because the Poush Mela would often take me back to Santiniketan. If he was unfamiliar with much that I was doing as an advertising artist, he kept track of me through my book designs. I knew what I was doing, made him happy. He showed this, not in words of praise, but in gifts of little sketches which he would draw on postcards while I sat by and talked of this and that.

He did, however, openly approve of *Pather Panchali*. I saw him in Calcutta shortly after the film was shown. He was to be treated for some eye trouble. "Your film gave me the feeling," he said, "that the camera may be the best medium through which to reveal Nature." Then he suggested a subject for me. "Make a film on a pilgrimage. Show how a group of people are thrown together on a common quest and what happens to them, individually, and in relation to each other." "But pilgrimages are not what they used to be," somebody commented. "They have lost their purity."

Master-mashai didn't look up from the sketch of a koi fish that he was doing for me. "It may seem sordid", he said, "if you're looking from a middle distance. If you get far enough away from it, it loses its ugliness. Or if you get close enough to it. I want him to get very close when he makes his film."

My last visit to Santiniketan was in 1961. Master-mashai was confined to his room — which was also his studio — struck with arthritis and barely able to move about. But as he had done ever since he took to painting, he was producing one sketch every day. He brought them for me to see. They were black and white sketches with occasional touches of colour here and there. One didn't think schools and traditions when one saw these paintings. They were the work of an artist at the prime of his life, who had lost the flexibility of limbs, but not the agility of mind, nor the visionary insight which can turn the most humdrum aspects of daily life into the stuff of art.

"I want to make a film about you — about you — about your paintings," I said hesitantly.

"But have you already made one about my Guru — Abanindranath?" he asked.

"No, not yet."

Master-mashai looked up and smiled.

"Well, that ought to come first, don't you think?

How can a shishya precede the Guru?"

THE LURE OF TERRACOTTA: A PIONEERING SCHOLAR'S UNTIMELY END

Published in *The Statesman*, 15 January 1972

The buzzer sounded. I opened the door to let in David McCutchion, just back from a fortnight's sojourn in the wilds of Orissa. He put his bicycle lamp down on the table and slumped down on the couch. "I'm exhausted", he said. He looked it too. The lean face was lined with fatigue, the deep tan was — with David — obviously not acquired on the beach at Puri, and his hair badly needed the barber's attention.

Three months earlier, David had come back from England with his hair down to his shoulders. We asked him if it was a concession to the Trend. David flicked off the notion with a dry laugh. "If you only knew how much a haircut costs in England these days!" Back in Calcutta, his hair was soon back to its original length. Then followed a month-long trip to during the Pujas to Madhya Pradesh, followed soon after by a Christmas visit to Orissa. No wonder the barber had again to be pushed into the background.

"Was it a good trip?" I asked. David hesitated, and I immediately regretted the casual way I had put my question. I should have known that David would scarcely bring himself to answer with a simple "yes" or "no", and thereby lay himself open to the charge of imprecision. David was a stickler for exactitude. He was also extremely sensitive to people and places. For him, every journey into temple country was a bundle of experiences ranging from the ridiculous to the sublime. How could he describe in one word, or even in a few words, what it was like? What he usually did was "tell all about it". The process took about an hour, and inevitably left one with the feeling that while David McCutchion was properly bent upon writing the definite treatise on the terracotta temples of Bengal, he shouldn't stop there, but go on to write about the other aspect — the purely human aspect — of his adventures. For adventures they truly were, with David as the hero, comic and tragic by turns, triumphant and despondent in equal measures. What a rich tapestry of anecdotes and experiences it would make!

A BRIEF MEETING

When David first arrived in Calcutta, I doubt if he even knew of the existence of terracotta temples in Bengal. And this in spite of his two years in Santiniketan in the heart of terracotta country. It was in Santiniketan that I first met him. It was a brief meeting — 1960 — and the only impression I retained was of dark hair and a sallow complexion. The second meeting was in Calcutta when David had given up his Santiniketan job and joined Jadavpur University as a reader in comparative literature. We found that we shared a love of Western classical music of the Baroque period. David began to drop in from time to time and we listened to music. I found that he knew some Bengali and was hoping to learn more. I needed help in translating the dialogue of my films into English for the purpose of subtitling. I asked David if he would do it. He readily agreed, saying it would give him opportunity to improve his Bengali. The first film he translated was *Teen Kanya*, and thereafter every film right down to my most recent one. He insisted on translating every word and getting all the nuances right, while I worried about all that reading matter getting in the way of the images. It took us half a dozen films and nearly as many years to come to a satisfactory compromise. It was while shooting *Abhijaan* in the starkly beautiful Birbhum countryside that I wrote to David in Calcutta suggesting that he should come down and spend a weekend with us. He turned up one January morning with his rucksack and we had no difficulty in putting him up in lordly style: we were staying in the palace of the Hetampur Raj. Next morning he came to the shooting site, hung about for a while, then suddenly disappeared. He came back late in the afternoon looking flushed and excited. "There are some temples around here", he announced, "with carvings of sahibs and memsahibs on them." I said the terracotta temples of Birbhum were well known. "I took some pictures," he added. I glanced at his modest camera and said, "If you need film we have plenty to spare."

That, I think, was the beginning of David McCutchion's interest in the terracotta temples of Bengal. Back in Calcutta, David borrowed my copy of Mukul Dey's book on the Birbhum temples. He brought it back a few days later and borrowed a nineteenth-century PWD publication, *The Ancient Monuments of Bengal*, and the Bengali *Banglai Bhraman* (Travelling in Bengal), an excellent two-volume guidebook published in the twenties by the East Bengal Railways. I suggested a few more places to visit for temples — Bishnupur of course, and Bansberia, Kalna, Guptipara, and so on. David went to all these places and brought back pictures. "Snaps" would be a better description of them. He was curious to know what the carvings portrayed. "That bird with the enormous beak, for instance," he would ask, "what is it?" I said it was the Bakasura, one of the several demons that Krishna had slain. I could see that David had found a new hobby. The question was how long it would last.

As it turned out, the hobby soon developed into a remorseless study at the deepest level, and lasted till the last conscious moment of his life. In a matter of weeks, David had finished reading whatever I was able to offer him from my bookshelves. Soon, weekends began to be consumed by trips into terracotta country. The snaps rapidly began to acquire a professional look; one could see that the photographer had waited for the most favourable play of sunlight on the sculptured surfaces. The modest camera was replaced by a sleek Leica complete with close-up lenses, and a metre to ensure correct exposure. Every trip into terracotta country was now followed by three visits to my house within a few days of each other — the first for a verbal description of the adventure, the second for an examination of the black-and-white enlargements, the third for a look at the colour slides, with David providing a running commentary. In a matter of months, our positions had smoothly and irrevocably reversed. It was now David who talked while I listened.

Apart from a survey of the known temples, every so often there was the discovery of unknown ones. No one had ever ventured as far afield in the pursuit of temples as David McCutchion, and this often yielded unexpected bonuses. It was perhaps, the growing conviction that he was a pioneer in an inadequately explored field that gave David the determination to carry the study in the most throughgoing manner possible. Since David was his own sponsor, he had to do it the hard way, always travelling third class by train, and, once in a temple country, cycling or walking — mostly the latter — often up to fifteen or twenty miles a day, frequently on the off-chance of finding a temple that some villager had told him was "over there".

As the study progressed, David's method of documentation became more and more meticulous. "But you've been to Midnapore before," I'd tell him, "Why d'you want to go again?" "You see", David would explain, "the temple at so-and-so faces east. The last time I was there the sun had already moved away and the east face was in the shadow. This time I've planned it so I can spend the night in the rest house, to get up at the crack of dawn, and ..."

But even twice was not enough, as he soon realized. The scale was important too. The temples had to be measured. So David bought himself a fifty foot measuring tape, went back again, and measured.

STYLISTIC ANTECEDENTS

These tours, one need hardly add, were not confined to West Bengal alone. He went twice to what was then East Pakistan. From Paharpur he brought back the first colour slides I had ever seen of the celebrated ruins of the Buddhist era.

Then there was the question of stylistic antecedents. There were temples in other parts of India that showed affinities with Bengal types. These naturally fell within David's orbit. So he went to Madhya Pradesh, to the south, to Rajasthan. These were even more of a challenge than the expeditions in Bengal, because David's knowledge of Hindi was confined to a dozen or so stock phrases. Still he was able to get around, find the temples, and bring back pictures and measurements. And of course, stories too. "Here was the temple in the desert, right in the middle of nowhere, looking obviously deserted. But as I approached it, I suddenly heard a flutter of wings, and a dozens of peacocks came charging out and went scuttling over the sand." Or the story about the night spent on a charpoy provided by the village headman and placed right in the middle of a hall in an

David McCutchion with Ray at his Lake Temple Road residence

eleventh-century temple in Bhopal. "I lay flat on my back and kept flashing my torch up at the ceiling and picking out the marvellous carvings."

His Hindi, too, improved over the years. "Daku hai, sahib! Mat jaiye!" he was warned once by some villagers at the point of launching on one of his excursions on foot in Madhya Pradesh. David knew he was being warned against the dacoits, but he went all the same. "I was sure I didn't look like a rich banya, and the bandits would never guess I was carrying expensive cameras in my bag." So David walked seven miles through the bandit country, found his temple and came back unscathed.

David's indignation at the neglect of temples was as deep as his despair at some of the drastic and tasteless attempts at their preservation. Both David and I loved Bakreswar with its weird proliferation of mouldy crumbled temples around holy hot springs. I went there first in 1962. When I returned two years later, I found all the temples had in the meantime been given a coating of whitewash and painted pink. This, I was told, was preservation. I reported this to David. He went promptly to check, came back, drafted a sizzling letter of protest, went round on his bike calling on "eminent intellectuals" and succeeded in persuading them to put their signatures to that letter. Only the other day, back from Madhya Pradesh, David poured his venom at a new kind of vandalism that he said was now rampant in the country. "They've started chopping off the heads of the figures from temples to sell them to tourists. I counted thirteen such heads missing from a single temple. I know they were there two years ago; I have pictures to prove it. Can you imagine anything more sickening? What is the world coming to?"

FIRST-RATE EXHIBITION

Another activity which was becoming more frequent of late was lecturing on temples to the accompaniment of colour slides. Even these brought forth a rich fund of stories. For instance, there was the talk arranged by X, a veritable bastion of Bengali culture. Pelting rain flooded the streets, and hardly a dozen people turned up. But David started his talk nevertheless. X sat in the front row and kept smiling and nodding her head. "Why, I'm making an impression! I thought", said David. "Then, at one point, I felt thirsty and turned to X and asked for a glass of water. She just kept smiling and nodding her head..."

Thousands of negatives, thousands of enlargements, thousands of color slides — each and every one of them numbered, described, classified and filed neatly away so that he could lay his hands on any one of them at a moment's notice. And there was the tape recorder which David was using to record the song of the "patuas". Study of "pata" painting had evolved as a natural by-product of the temples, and David, had already had to his credit a first-rate exhibition of "patua" scrolls at Calcutta's Bangiya Sahitya Parishad. It is most probable that he would have launched on a definite study of 'pata' and 'patuas' immediately after finishing his work on the temples.

The only book that David was able to see partly through the press was an eighty-page monograph on the terracotta temples ("a guidebook, really") which the Asiatic Society will publish. He was pleased with the book, but kept worrying about the typography. "You see, the trouble is, there are some pages in the text which demand, for the sake of clarity, as many as six variations of emphasis in the typography. At the same time, I don't want the pages to become a hodge-podge of typefaces..."

"Nothing exasperates me more than irrationality," David used to say. And what with his frequent encounters with museum officials, railway booking clerks, customs personnel, keepers of holy temples, self-styled patrons of the arts, and zealous members of the police force (a rich story here about being hauled up as a Chinese spy), David surely had far more legitimate reasons to wax eloquent over irrationality than most other people. But what, one wonders — thinking of the circumstances — could be more irrational in the scheme of things than the death of David McCutchion himself?

PANKAJ KUMAR MALLIK

Obituary quote in *Amrita Bazar Patrika*, 22 February 1978

Pankaj Mallik earned legendary fame and popularity as a singer and teacher of Rabindrasangeet. He devoted his whole life to this cause — using the medium of the film, the radio and the gramophone — and succeeded in endearing himself to the music-loving Indians all over the country.

Satyajit Ray
22 February 1978

BANSI CHANDRAGUPTA

Published in *Festival News* (News Bulletin of Filmostsav 1982), 10 January 1982

Ray with Bansi on the sets of *Jana Aranya*.
Photograph by Sandip Ray

Bansi Chandragupta's death in his prime has been a major tragedy for Indian films. We two had the habit of making Sunday outings into the countryside and were fans of Bresson. He took still photos almost continuously. Bansi after months of hard work finally selected the right cottage for Harihar in *Pather Panchali*. Then later, when we were working for *Aparajito*, Bansi built the house for Harihar in the studios, which had the perfect quality of a rural setting.

Equally convincing was his urban setting. The upper-class set for *Charulata* bore witness to his grasp over ornate sets.

I know Bansi from 1943, when the Jammu born young man came down to Calcutta with the intention of learning painting from Nandalal Bose at Santiniketan. In fact, he went over to Santiniketan, but somehow he did not get admission and came back to Calcutta. He was a gifted painter who took an unusual interest in films. In 1947, we formed the Calcutta Film

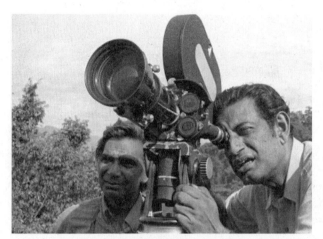

Ray and Bansi shooting outdoors.
Photograph by Nemai Ghosh, courtesy Satyaki Ghosh

Society when Bansi was working for a Bengali film. So great was his creative abilities that when Renoir came down to Calcutta in 1949 to film *The River* and Bansi was asked to assist him, Renoir in course of shooting, made his own art director the production designer and asked Bansi to be his art director.

Bansi, throughout his career, was an indefatigable worker and very much a perfectionist. He left for Bombay in 1970 but came back to help me when I wanted him for *Shatranj Ke Khiladi*. That film was the summit of his achievement.

As far as I could collect from him, Bansi was not too happy with the work there. His loving care for his work was not appreciated in Bombay. Bombay wanted expensive sets. Only during the last few years of his life, when the new film-makers were making good films on a low budget, did he derive some satisfaction from his work.

STATEMENT ON THE DEATH OF MARIE SETON

Published in *Sunday Observer*, 14 April 1984

I t is difficult to believe that Marie Seton is no more; she had always seemed to me to be more alive than most people I could think of. Her boundless energy was mostly spent on causes that she believed in, and what she believed in was what all right-minded and conscientious, people believe in. Of late, Marie had grown physically frail, but her mind was as alert and probing as ever.

It is difficult to believe that Marie Seton is no more; she had always seemed to me to be more alive than most people I could think of. Her boundless energy was mostly spent on causes that she believed in, and what she believed in was what all right-minded and conscientious people believe in. Of late, Marie had grown physically frail, but her mind was as alert and probing as ever.

I met Marie for the first time in the mid-fifties when she came to Calcutta to lecture on the cinema. I was already full of admiration for the zestful Englishwoman for her pioneering study of Eisenstein, and was most anxious to meet her. We met in her hotel room. I wanted to talk about the Soviet master, but Marie had just seen Pather Panchali in Delhi, and wished to talk of nothing else. I casually mentioned that the film was supposed to go to the Cannes festival, but some officials in New Delhi didn't welcome the idea of an Indian film showing poverty being sent abroad. Marie at once produced note paper and dashed off a letter to the then Minister of Information & Broadcasting, urging him to intervene and make sure that the film was sent to Cannes.

This was typical of Marie. She was never content merely to feel strongly about a cause; she had to do something about it, even if it meant sticking her neck out. And all her life she never lacked cuses to fight for. Any form of social inequity — no matter in which part of the world it occured — upset her to the core of her being. She also took it as a cause to spread the gospel of good cinema, and made countless trips to all corners of the globe to do so. It is largely due to her pioneering zeal that the film society movement spread and took roots in our own country.

A few months before her own death, Marie suffered one of the greatest shocks of her life in the way Mrs Gandhi's life ended. Marie had long been a friend of the Nehru family, and 'Indu' had been especially close to her. But Marie was not content merely to sit and suffer; till the day before she died , she was writing and advising on projects to perpetuate her friend's memory.

As for Marie's own memory, it will certainly stay undimmed in the minds of those who were fortunate enough to know her as a friend.

Marie Seton with Satyajit and Bijoya Ray
at her London residence

I met Marie for the first time in the mid-fifties when she came to Calcutta to lecture on the cinema. I was already full of admiration for the zestful Englishwoman for her pioneering study of Eisenstien, and was most anxious to meet her. We met in her hotel room. I wanted to talk about the Soviet master, but Marie had just seen *Pather Panchali* in Delhi, and wished to talk of nothing else. I casually mentioned that the film was supposed to go to the Cannes Festival, but some officials in New Delhi didn't welcome the idea of an Indian film showing poverty being sent abroad. Marie at once produced a note paper and dashed off a letter to the then Minister of Information and Broadcasting, urging him to intervene and make sure that the film was sent to Cannes.

This was typical of Marie. She was never content merely to feel strongly about a cause; she had to do something about it, even if it meant sticking her neck out. And all her life she never lacked causes to fight for. Any form of social inequity — no matter in which part of the world it occurred — upset her to the core of her being. She also took it as a cause to spread the gospel of good cinema, and made countless trips to all corners of the globe to do so. It is largely due to her pioneering zeal that the film society movement spread and took root in our own country.

A few months before her own death, Marie suffered one of the greatest shocks of her life in the way Mrs. Gandhi's life ended. Marie had long been a friend of the Nehru family, and "Indu" had been especially close to her. But Marie was not content merely to sit and suffer; till the day before she died, she was writing and advising on projects to perpetuate her friend's memory.

As for Marie's own memory, it will certainly stay undimmed in the minds of those who were fortunate enough to know her as a friend.

NEMAI GHOSH

From *Nemai Ghosh: a monograph*, Sunipa Basu, National Film Archive of India, 2009

We founded the Calcutta Film Society in 1947 with the help of a few friends and associates. Nemai Ghosh was one of them. Like me, he was also enamoured by the cinema; so we got along very well. I was a mere cineaste then but he was already a practitioner as a cameraman. However, he harboured the desire to direct films himself at the back of his mind. The chance came his way during the late forties when he made *Chhinnamool* on the theme of Partition. It was the first instance of realism in Bengali cinema. But thereafter he was compelled to head for Madras for want of work in Calcutta, and had to spend the rest of his life there. Being a leftist to the core, he did a lot for the cinema workers in Madras. We exchanged correspondence only occasionally. But whenever we met, the old warmth of friendship was revived. Today I am feeling his absence intensely and I am sure the cineworkers of Madras are also feeling likewise.

Nemai Ghosh speaking at a Film Society meeting as Ray looks on

Ray with the Golden Lion at Venice, 1957

FESTIVAL GREETINGS

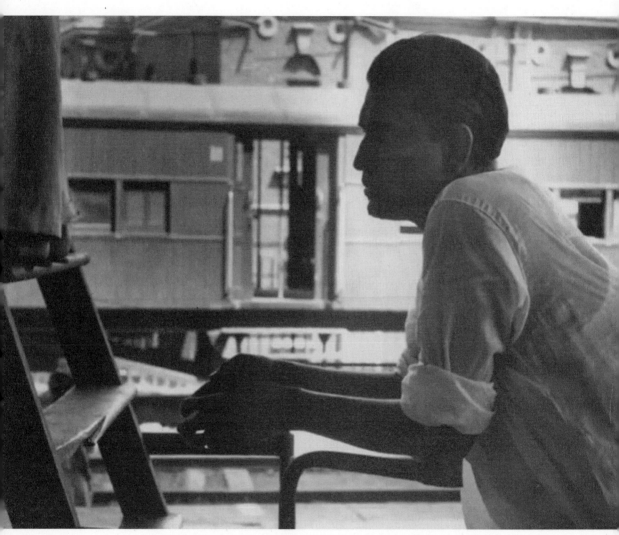
Ray during the shooting of *Aparajito*, 1956. Photograph courtesy Magnum Photos

A WORD FROM
THE DIRECTOR

Bharatiya Natya Sangha souvenir on the Apu Trilogy, New Delhi, 1969

When in the year 1953 I set about making *Pather Panchali*, the idea of a trilogy was far from my thoughts. My horizon did not — indeed, in the circumstances in which the film was made, it could not — extend beyond one film.

The two books by Bibhutibhushan Banerji on which the trilogy was based, had existed since the 1930s. *Pather Panchali* was a milestone and a masterpiece. In 1947, I accepted an assignment to provide illustrations for a new edition of the book, and it was while doing this that I was struck by the filmic quality of some of its episodes. They stayed at the back of my mind for five years and grew into a film scenario. The shooting begun in 1953. I had a job in an advertising agency at the time and was obliged to keep it lest the film should prove a fiasco. Work on the film had therefore to be confined to Sundays and holidays.

Pather Panchali was finished in 1955. It was an instant success. I gave up my desk job and plunged into film-making.

There were two things about *Aparajito* that drew me to it. The book itself was rambling and formless, but like all of Bibhutibhushan's work, it was shot through with a deep humanism. The first part of the book was laid in Benaras — this was a tempting bail, what more photogenic locale is there in the world? Secondly, and more importantly, there was the relationship between an unsophisticated widowed mother and her ambitious city-educated son who grows inevitably away from her. At one point in the story,

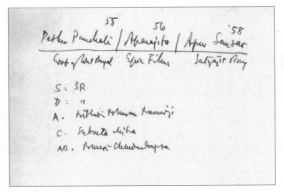

Scribblings on the Apu Trilogy from Ray's Notebook

Bibhutibhushan describes the feelings of the boy upon receiving the news of the mother's death. The immediate reaction, says the author, is one of relief, of a freedom from bondage. This seemed to me to plumb the depths of truth, and it would not be untrue to say that the whole scenario of *Aparajito* was an exploration of the mother and son relationship on the basis of this one profound revelation.

Aparajito flopped in India. While making it, I had toyed with the idea of a trilogy. I now banished Apu from my thoughts and quickly made a comedy. But for the success of *Aparajito* abroad, the third part would never have been made.

Apur Sansar is freely adapted from the second half of the book, *Aparajito*. Once again the mainspring of the film is contained in one striking situation in the book. Apu's wife dies in childbirth. The child survives. But Apu, subconsciously holding the boy responsible for his wife's death, declines to accept the responsibilities of fatherhood. The story ends, however, on a note of triumphant reconciliation.

Whether or not the three films made up a cohesive whole, I do not know. I have not had the opportunity to see them in their proper order. But as the maker of the trilogy, I can at least vouch for the singleness of their aim, which is to depict human beings in relation to one another and to their particular milieus with honesty and sympathy.

FOREWORD TO SATYAJIT RAY FILM FESTIVAL: THE SECOND DECADE

Foreword to the souvenir published on occasion of 'Satyajit Ray Film Festival: The Second Decade', held from 2 to 8 May 1979, Kolkata

Critics have often accused me of a grasshopperish tendency to jump from theme to theme, from genre to genre, in a succession of films, rather than pursue one dominant subject in an easily recognizable style which would help them to pigeonhole me and affix me with a label. This diversity is brought more sharply into focus in a retrospective such as the present one, where works spread over a number of years are brought together and viewed in close succession. A whodunit, a children's fantasy, a tale of adventure, problems of contemporary urban youth, the famine of 1943, all made over a ten-year stretch — it's inevitable that a feeling of restlessness, perhaps even if indecision, will emerge from this jumble.

All I can say in defense, if one is needed, is that this diversity faithfully reflects my own personality, and that behind every film lies a cool decision. In my case, the urge to make films is

Cover of the souvenir

also very often an urge to venture into areas which others at home have often avoided, or gone over clumsily or curiously. In other words, one of my main preoccupations has been exploration and expansion of arable land rather than concentration on one crop in one field. Even my first film *Pather Panchali* was actuated as much by a desire to break new grounds as to film a classic novel. After all, many major novels had been filmed before my time.

Goopy Gyne Bagha Byne and *Sonar Kella* are also attempts to explore new territory. *Chiriakhana*, too — although it was a subject which was thrust upon me — was taken up in the spirit of investing a Western genre with an indigenous character. Perhaps I should add here that I do not turn up my nose at "popular" genres, owing, as I do, some of my most cherished moments in the cinema to them. Also, I do not believe that popularity is incompatible either with seriousness or with Art.

Even though diverse, I hope perceptive viewers will discover links between the films — links of style, of craftsmanship and, most importantly, of attitude.

MESSAGE FOR THE BOKARO FILM SOCIETY

The Bokaro Film Society are holding an Eisenstein Film Festival and are launching a journal called *Film Sense* on this occasion.

I send my heartiest good wishes to both the society and the journal and wish them continued success.

Satyajit Ray
5 July 1982

The facsimile of the message written to
The Bokaro Film Society by Ray dated 5 July 1982

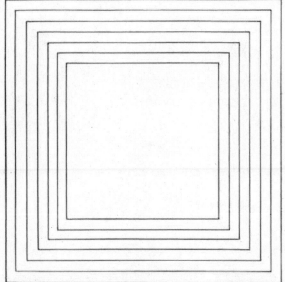

filmotsav 82

Calcutta 3-17 January 82

Cover of the brochure of Filmotsav 82

EXCERPT OF ADDRESS, FILMOTSAV 82

Excerpt from the address delivered by Ray on the Opening Ceremony of Filmotsav 82
held at Kolkata from 3 to 17 January, 1982

I've been looking forward to this for a long time. I am fully aware that Calcutta makes a rude assault on the sensibilities of people who come here for the first time. An American guidebook cites it as the city in the world most to be avoided. Yet, the poeple's friendliness, the public's response to cultural phenomenon of all kinds — is enormous here. I hope that some of our visitors will remain long enough to reach the point where they will start admiring this city.

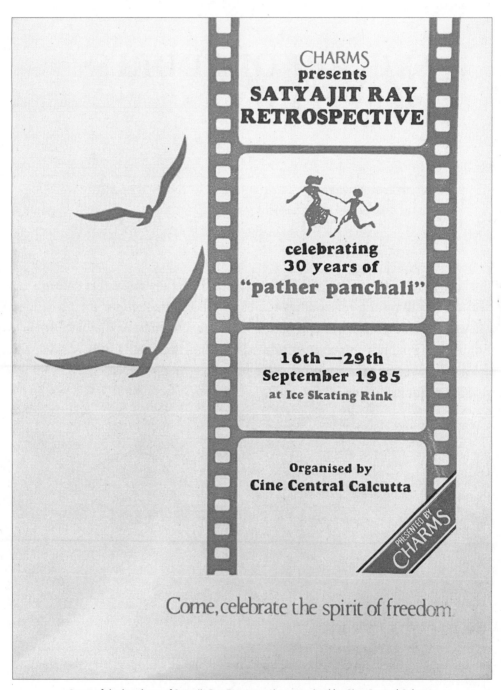

Cover of the brochure of Satyajit Ray Retrospective organized by Cine Central Calcutta

MESSAGE FOR CINE CENTRAL RETROSPECTIVE

Message by Ray for Satyajit Ray Retrospective celebrating 30 years of *Pather Panchali* organized by Cine Central from 16 to 29 September 1985

SATYAJIT RAY

Cine Central are holding a retrospective of my films I convey my best wishes to them on the occasion.

12/9/85

The facsimile of the message written to the organizers by Ray dated 12 September 1985

C ine Central are holding a retrospective of my films. I convey my best wishes to them on the occasion.

Satyajit Ray

12 September 1985

MESSAGE FOR FFSI SHORT FILM AND DOCUMENTARY FILM FESTIVAL

Message on occasion of the Festival of Short Films and Documentaries jointly organized by The Federation of Film Societies of India and Seagull Film Society from 2 to 8 March 1985 at Kolkata

I an happy to know that The Federation of Film Societies and the Seagull Film Society Calcutta are jointly organizing a festival of shorts and documentaries in Calcutta during March 2–8, 1985.

Short films, which use their own unique language of expression, can provide keen aesthetic pleasure as well as educative analyses of important social and political problems. Little attempt has so far been made in our country to focus attention on this important aspect of film making. I hope the present festival will succeed in doing so. I wish it all success and request all concerned to give a helping hand to the organizers.

Satyajit Ray
25 January 1985

I am happy to know that the Federation of Film Societies and the Seagull Film Society, Calcutta are jointly organising a festival of shorts and documentaries in Calcutta during March 2-8, 1985.

Short films, which use their own unique language of expression, can provide keen aesthetic pleasure as well as educative analyses of important social and political problems. Little attempt has so far been made in our country to focus attention on this important aspect of film making. I hope the present festival will succeed in doing so. I wish it all success and request all concerned to give a helping hand to the organisers.

Satyajit Ray

25/1/85.

MESSAGE FOR BIMAL ROY RETROSPECTIVE

Message in the brochure of the Retrospective of Bimal Roy's films held in
November, 1986 at Kolkata

In the initial stages of his film career, Bimal Roy was a cameraman. His transformation into a director was as unexpected as it was significant. Indian Cinema in the early forties was dominated by the theatre. The acting was stage-oriented, the dialogue was theatrical and even the disposition of actors within the frame was theatrical. With his very first film *Udayer Pathey* (*Hamrahi* in Hindi), Bimal Roy was able to sweep aside the cobwebs of the old tradition and introduce a realism and subtlety that was wholly suited to the cinema. He was thus "undoubtedly a pioneer". He reached his peak with a film that still reverberates in the minds of those who saw it when it was first made. I refer to *Do Bigha Zamin*, which remains one of the landmarks of Indian Cinema.

Fairly early in his career, Bimal Roy moved to Bombay and settled there. His contribution to Hindi cinema was most distinguished.

MESSAGE FOR FILMOTSAV 86

Letter to the organizers of the Filmotsav organized by The Film Festival Directorate,
Government of India in 1986 at Hyderabad

The Filmotsav organized by the Film Festival Directorate, Government of India, has been an important annual feature of the Indian film scene ever since the first International Competitive Festival was held in New Delhi in 1965.

This year the Filmotsav — a non-competitive festival comprising prizewinners from other festivals, along with a selection of films from all over the world — is being held in Hyderabad, which is a worthy venue being, I understand, a very film-conscious city.

As usual, an important feature of Filmotsav will be the Indian Panorama — a showcase for the most noteworthy films made during the present year by our own filmmakers from all over the country.

All in all, an occasion to look forward to. I send my cordial greetings to Filmotsav and wish it all the success it deserves.

Seven Decades Of Bengali Cinema

Seven Decades Of Bengali Cinema

NANDAN

**West Bengal Film Centre
Calcutta**

Published on the occasion of the Exhibition on
Bengali Cinema during International Film Festival
of India
January 10-20, 1990

Cover and first page of the brochure of International Film Festival, 1990

MESSAGE FOR INTERNATIONAL FILM FESTIVAL, 1990

Message to the organizers of the International Film Festival of India in 1990 at Kolkata

The film lovers of Calcutta must be very happy that the International Film festival of India is being held in this city after a gap of 8 years. The Festival opens on January 10.

An exhibition to highlight 70 years of Bengali cinema will be held at Nandan and a booklet on the same theme published during the festival.

May I convey my best wishes for the success of both the undertakings.

Satyajit Ray
5 January 1990

The facsimile of the message written to the organizers by Ray dated 5 January 1990

MESSAGE FOR RETROSPECTIVE OF LESTER JAMES PERIES

Brochure of Retrospective of Lester James Peries Films organized by Cine Central
from 7 to 31 December 1990 at Globe Cinema, Kolkata

I am extremely sorry that I cannot be present at the inauguration of the Retrospective of Lester James Peries's films organized by Cine Central, Calcutta. I have been looking forward to this event for a very long time. Unfortunately, I have just started working on a new film which has a very tight schedule, and therefore leaves time for very little else.

Lester and I have been friends for over thirty years. We started our film careers about the same time — he with *Rekava* and I with *Pather Panchali*. Luckily, both the films won recognition at home and abroad, and neither of us has looked back since then. It's a pity that very few of Lester's films have come my way, but I know he has produced a large body of significant work both in Singhalese and English.

I wish him all success in the first retrospective of his films held in Calcutta.

May I also extend a warm welcome to Sumitra, Lester's wife, who has always edited Lester's films and is now established as a film-maker herself.

Satyajit Ray

MESSAGE FOR INTERNATIONAL SHORT FILM FESTIVAL, DHAKA

Message to the organizers of the 2nd International Short Film Festival, Dhaka, January 1991

SATYAJIT RAY

The facsimile of the message written to the organizers by Ray dated 5 January 1991

Bangladesh Short Film Forum are holding their second international short film festival at Dhaka. This is an admirable enterprise, as not enough weight is given to this important field of cinematic experience. I send my warm good wishes for the success of the festival.

Satyajit Ray
5 January 1991

MESSAGE FOR DOCUMENTARY FILM FESTIVAL, 1992

Message for International Documentary Film Festival, Bombay, 1992

I am indeed sorry that my health does not permit me to give an interview for the Bombay International Documentary Film Festival. However, in view of the importance of the documentary as a medium and as a vital force in the cinema, such a move as a festival is surely welcome.

I wish the festival all success.

Satyajit Ray
26 January 1992

Ray with his teacher Benode Behari Mukherjee during the making of *Inner Eye*, 1972. Photograph by Sandip Ray

Ray's draft for the Apu Trilogy
LP cover and the final LP cover

LP SLEEVE
NOTES

Ray in a pensive mood. Photograph by Nemai Ghosh, courtesy Satyaki Ghosh

THE STORY, THE MUSIC

Songs and Music by Satyajit Ray from the film Goopy Gyne & Bagha Byne,
LP Sleeve note, 1969

THE STORY

Goopy Gyne was originally a twenty-page short story which my grandfather wrote for the children's magazine that he founded just before the outbreak of the First World War. I knew and loved the story as a child, and when, in 1960, we decided to revive the magazine, one of the first stories we reprinted from the early issues was *Goopy Gyne*.

The story describes the adventures of two village youngsters, Goopy and Bagha, who are given three boons by a benign King of Ghosts. One of these gives them the power to hold people spellbound with their singing and drumming (Goopy is the singer, and Bagha the drummer). Another provides them with magic shoes, by means of which they transport themselves to the kingdom of Shundi, where the good king appoints them court musicians. Soon the bad king of Halla declares war on Shundi. Anxious for the safety of their peace-loving patron, Goopy and Bagha journey to Halla as spies and, largely with the aid of their music, prevent the war, bring the two kings together, and marry their two daughters.

THE MUSIC

The film is freely adapted from the original, keeping the main lines of the plot, but adding new turns and twists mainly to provide Goopy and Bagha with opportunities for singing and drumming. Four out of seven songs sung by Goopy (with occasional vocal embellishments by Bagha) have more than a tinge of Bengali folk music in their rhythm and melody (Song Nos. 6 and 9 of Side I; 8 and 9 of Side II). Of the others, No. 5 of Side I is based on the classical morning raga Bhairavi. The accompaniment here consists of a tanpura, two sitars, and a bamboo flute. Song No. 3 of Side II parodies the south Indian Carnatic style of singing, and uses, along with a trumpet and violins, the classical south Indian string instrument called the veena.

Most of the orchestral pieces use a combination of Eastern and Western instruments: violins, cellos, electric guitar, trumpet, trombone, xylophone and vibraphone, as well as sitar, sarod, Indian flute and Indian percussion.

There are two items on this disc which were not composed by me. The first is the music that goes with the Dance of the Ghosts. This is a straight reproduction of a form of percussion quartet popular in south India. The four instruments are the classical mridanga, the popular ganjira, the sharp-sounding ghatam — which is nothing more than a claypot — and the quaint, twangy mursing, a tiny instrument which is held between the teeth and plucked with the forefinger. The other item is the beautiful flute melody on Side II. This I heard being played by a camel driver in Rajasthan: two flutes played simultaneously from the two corners of the mouth, one holding the drone and the other weaving the melody around it.

ASHESH BANDOPADHYAYA PLAYS ESRAJ

Ashesh Bandopadhyaya Plays Esraj, LP Sleeve note, 1978

One of my lasting memories of Santiniketan, where I was a student some thirty-five years ago, is of an unassuming young man of almost diminutive stature playing the esraj as I have not heard it playing before or since. This instrument, so closely linked with Bengal and the Bengali song, is a smaller version of the dilruba. Having fewer sympathetic strings than its elder brother, the esraj produces a softer and mellower tone. As such it comes into its own only in the hands of the master whose command of the melodic line can make up for the instrument's lack of tonal colour. I doubt if the esraj has been heard to better advantage in our time than in the hands of Ashesh Bandopadhyaya. When I heard him in Santiniketan, Ashesh Bandopadhyaya was not much in evidence as a soloist, but he was always on hand to provide the accompaniments to recitals of Rabindrasangeet. Such was his command of the instrument, and so deep and true his feelings for the songs, that one often found oneself listening to the instrument rather than the singer.

Ray's note and signature on LP sleeve of
Ashesh Bandopadhyaya Plays Esraj

Ashesh Bandopadhyaya was born in a family of musicians belonging to the illustrious Bishnupur gharana. He is the fourth and youngest son of Ramprasanna Bandopadhyaya, himself a fine musician and the first teacher of Ashesh. True to family traditions, Ashesh was given lessons both in vocal and instrumental music. When, at the age of nine, he lost his father, Ashesh left Bishnupur and came to Calcutta to continue his studies under uncles Gopeshwar and Surendranath, both of whom made enormous contributions to the spread of classical music in Bengal.

Ashesh kept up his study of the esraj and sitar under Surendranath, making rapid strides and winning top prizes in national contests while still in his teens. In 1937, when he was seventeen, Gopeshwar sent him to Santiniketan at the behest of Rabindranath, who was looking for teachers of classical music for Sangit Bhavana. Ashesh has lived in Santiniketan ever since, perfecting his own music and taking active part in the musical life of the institution.

The present record, Ashesh Bandopadhyaya's first solo contribution to the gramophone, perpetuates his art of playing classical ragas on the esraj.

MUSIC FROM THE APU TRILOGY

Ravi Shankar: Music from Satyajit Ray's Apu Trilogy, LP Sleeve note, 1978

P*ather Panchali* was still in production when I wrote to Ravi Shankar in Delhi asking him to compose the music for the film. I was an admirer of his music for the ballet *Discovery of India*, and was also familiar with some of the work he had done for films. Ravi Shankar agreed readily. However, when the time came to record the music, he was in the middle of a concert tour. There was no question of postponement, as we were faced with a released deadline, and certainly no question of replacing the composer. In the end Ravi Shankar managed to come down for a day, was rushed to the projection room to be shown half of the film in a roughly edited version, and in the same afternoon composed and recorded the music in a single session ending in the small hours of the next morning.

One of the first things that Ravi Shankar did when I met him shortly after his arrival in Calcutta was to hum a line of melody which he said had occurred to him as a possible theme for the film. It was a simple tune with a wistful, pastoral quality which seemed to suit exactly the mood of the film. It went on to become the main motif of *Pather Panchali*.

Since I felt that in the short time that I had it would be too constricting for Ravi Shankar to have to compose to precise, predetermined footages, the method we used was to decide on the mood and instrumental combination for a particular scene, and then provide music well beyond the required length. In addition, we recorded about half-a-dozen three-minute pieces on the sitar in various ragas and tempos. This took care of the risk of running short at the time of fitting the music to the scenes in the cutting room.

This is by no means an ideal method, but it has its advantages. For instance, the music that accompanies the ballet of the waterbugs in the film was originally played as one of the several variations on the main theme with no specific scenes in mind. In fact, there was no scene of dancing insects in the film at this stage; it grew out of the music in the cutting room.

It was decided at the outset not to use any Western instruments in *Pather Panchali*. In addition to the sitar, we used the dilruba, the bhimraj (elder brother of the esraj), the sarod and the pakhawaj.

The same instruments, played solo and in various combinations, were used in *Aparajito*. Once again we had a hectic recording session, with Ravi Shankar humming, strumming, improvising and instructing at a feverish pace, and the indefatigable flautist-cum-assistant Aloke Dey transcribing the composer's ideas into Indian notation and dealing out the foolscap sheets to the tense handful who had to keep plucking and bowing and thumping with scarcely a breathing space.

In *Apur Sansar*, Ravi Shankar had to contend with a story that was much more varied in texture than the first two films of the trilogy. It begins in a squalid North Calcutta setting, shifts to the countryside for Apu's wedding, comes back to Calcutta and, after the death of Apu's wife, accompanies the disconsolate hero on his wanderings from seaside to sylvan woods, to the wild and hilly coalmining areas of Chhota Nagpur, returning finally to the Bengal countryside for the concluding scenes. Five Indian instruments were obviously inadequate to cope with all this, so Ravi Shankar decided to add violins and cellos (even a piano for one particular piece). Also, the usual hectic one-day session was abandoned, and the music was composed and recorded over three days.

RITU GUHA — SONGS OF RABINDRANATH

Ritu Guha — Songs of Rabindranath, LP Sleeve note, 1981

Much of what passes for Rabindrasangeet these days, are flat, run-of-the mill recitals where, if one recognizes the words and the melodies, one looks in vain for the spirit. Rabindranath himself pleaded against what he called the

সংগীত-পরিচালনা/শুভ গুহ ঠাকুরতা
RITU GUHA • Songs of Rabindranath

Much of what passes for Rabindrasangeet these days are flat, run-of-the-mill recitals where, if one recognises the words and the melodies, one looks in vain for the spirit. Rabindranath himself pleaded against what he called the steamroller tactics of inept singers crushing the life out of his songs. To make them live, he asked that they be sung with feeling. The ideal, of course, is that feeling should go hand in hand with a limpid voice and a command over diction whereby the words, so important in Rabindrasangeet, would be given their due weight.

Few singers combine these qualities in such full measure as Ritu Guha. In listening to her one feels that she should have pleased the composer himself. One can pay her no greater tribute.

This is Ritu's first album of Rabindrasangeet, the first, one hopes, of many more to come.

Satyajit Ray

Left: LP Cover of *Ritu Guha — Songs of Rabindranath*;
Right: Part of the LP sleeve showing Ray's note

steamroller tactics of inept singers crushing the life out of his songs. To make them live he asked, that they be sung with feelings. The ideal, of course, is that the feeling should go hand in hand with a limpid voice and a command over diction whereby the words, so important in Rabindrasangeet, would be given their due weight.

Few singers combine this quality in such full measures as Ritu Guha. In listening to her one feels that she should have pleased the composer himself. One can pay her no greater tribute.

This is Ritu's first album of Rabindrasangeet, the first, one hopes, of many more to come.

THE ENCHANTED FLUTE
— ALOKENATH DEY

The Enchanted Flute — Alokenath Dey, LP sleeve note, 1982

LP sleeve of Alokenath Dey — *The Enchanted Flute* showing Ray's note

I have watched the development of Alokenath Dey as a flautist over the last 25 years. He played the haunty theme which Ravi Shankar wrote for *Pather Panchali* and he played all the flute passages in *Hirok Rajar Deshey*, having been my right-hand man on recording sessions on all my films in the intervening years.

Aloke's first LP is a demonstration of his virtuosity as well as his gifts as a composer. The music, which remains on a popular level, ranges from Bengali folk to Western Polka with a nod at Rabindrasangeet en route in some pieces Aloke plays as many as three separate flute parts, which are blended into an ensemble by the recording engineer.

There is much to enjoy in the *The Enchanted Flute*, not the least of which is the introduction it affords to a flautist of skill and experience.

AJOY CHAKRAVARTY

Ajoy Chakravarty, LP Sleeve note, 1985

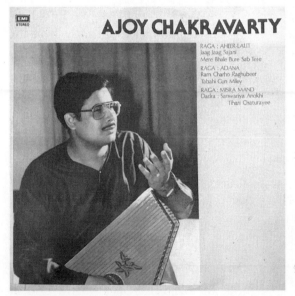

Over the years, great musicians have come and gone. The passing of every great one — singer, dancer, instrumentalist — gives rise to the anxious thought: Will there ever be another one like the one we have lost?

Actually, the void can never be filled, because true greatness implies a uniqueness, an inimitability. So we will never again have the likes of Faiaz Khan, Ghulam Ali Khan, Amir Khan, Kesarbai Kerker.

But if the world of music becomes poorer by the passing away of all-time greats, it must correspondingly be enriched by the often unheralded emergence of a stella nova, a new star, who arrives armed with the gifts of musicianship that makes him shine with a special brilliance in a highly competitive field. Such a star is Ajoy Chakravarty. Ajoy has not only the good fortune to possess a voice that his own untiring efforts have endowed him with an extraordinary depth and

AJOY CHAKRAVARTY

Over the years, great musicians have come and gone. The passing of every great one—singer, dancer, instrumentalist—gives rise to the anxious thought : Will there ever be another one like the one we have lost ? Actually, the void can never be filled, because true greatness implies a uniqueness, an inimitability. So we will never again have the likes of Faiaz Khan, Ghulam Ali Khan, Amir Khan, Kesarbai Kerkar.

But if the world of music becomes poorer by the passing away of all-time greats, it must correspondingly be enriched by the often unheralded emergence of a *stella nova*, a new star who arrives armed with the gifts of musicianship that make him shine with a special brilliance in a highly competitive field. Such a star is Ajoy Chakravarty. Ajoy has not only the good fortune to possess a voice that his own untiring efforts have endowed with an extraordinary depth and flexibility, but he has acquired that rarest of gifts—a mastery of form. In other words, Ajoy knows when to stop.

I have no doubt that Ajoy Chakravarty, who has already come a long way and displayed an admirable eclecticism, has much further to go along the path of the truly great.

Satyajit Ray

Part of the LP sleeve showing Ray's note

flexibility, but he has also acquired the rarest of gifts — a mastery of form. In other words, Ajoy knows when to stop.

I have no doubt that Ajoy Chakravarty, who has already come a long way and displayed an admirable eclecticism, has much further to go along the path of the truly great.

Ray at his Lake Temple Road residence

MISCELLANEOUS WRITINGS

Ray directing the opera *Valmiki-Prativa* for the documentary, *Rabindranath Tagore*, 1961. Photograph by Amanul Haq

CALCUTTA YOUTH CHOIR

President's message Calcutta Youth Choir's 4th Annual Function Bulletin, 16 May 1963

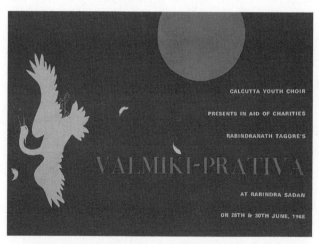

Brochure of Calcutta Youth Choir designed by Ray for their rendition of Tagore's *Vakmiki Prativa* in 1968

S tarted in 1959 as a sister organization to the Bombay Youth Choir, the Calcutta Youth Choir is a non-profit, non-professional organization which strives to revive and resuscitate the folk music of India. In addition to its rich repertoire of folk songs, the choir sings Vedic hymns as well as some of the best loved songs of Rabindranath, Atulprasad and Dilip Roy. Dances also form a necessary and colourful adjunct.

To commemorate the Choir's first anniversary a show was held at the New Empire Theatre in August 1960 in the presence of His Excellency the Governor of West Bengal and the total sale proceeds were handed over to His Excellency the Governor for the Assam Relief Fund.

In the year 1961 the Choir again held its annual show at the same theatre in the presence of His Excellency the Governor of West Bengal when it staged Tagore's *Valmiki*

Prativa to celebrate the Tagore Centenary and the total sale proceeds were donated to the Tagore Centenary Committee and Bihar Relief Fund.

In the year 1962 the Choir could not hold its annual show due to National Emergency — but it did many charity programmes for the NDF organized by the NDF Aid Committee and extra radio programmes.

This year it will hold its annual programme at the Rabindra Sarobar Stadium Hall on the 16th, 17th and 18th May in the evenings. They will present a programme of 'Folk Songs and Dances of India' on one day — Tagore's *Valmiki Prativa* on another and lastly they will present a very fine group of folk singers from Bihar and local folk artists.

The Choir will do this programme for the expansion of the Choir's activities.

Response from well-wishers and collaborators, and the organizers of this show has been overwhelmingly kind. We have received very encourteous co-operation in the matter of booking advertisement space in this brochure. Lastly, the Calcutta Youth Choir (C.Y.C.) tenders its deep gratitude and appreciation to The Magadh Sangh of Bihar, Moghai Ojha of Assam and local folk artists and Smt. Sumita Bhattacharjee for participating in this show.

MESSAGE FOR SCI-FI CINE CLUB

President's message for Science Fiction Cine Club brochure, 26 January 1966

H aving been a science-fiction addict for close on thirty years, the idea of the formation of a SF cine club has obvious appeal for me. I am happy to be associated with the club, which may very well be one of the first of its kind — here or abroad. On the occasion of the club's inauguration, may I wish its members many exciting and thought-provoking sessions of the best SF films from all over the world.

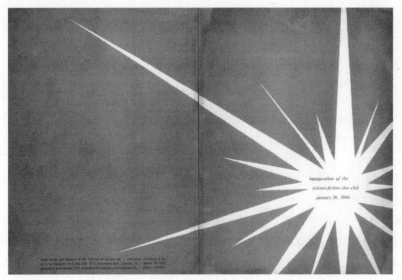

Science-fiction Cine-Club brochure designed by Ray

MAHANAGAR

Introduction to the translated English version of *Mahanagar* by Narendranath Mitra, Translated by S.K. Chatterjee and M.F. Franda, Jaico Publishing House, Bombay, 1968

Whu hen I read my first batch of Narendranath Mitra stories some fifteen years ago, I was struck by their acute observation of middle-class life. The field was narrow, familiar and even humdrum, and yet the yield was unusually rich and varied. Only a high degree of sensitivity and observation could achieve this.

Narendranath Mitra

Ever since then I have kept hunting out his stories in weeklies, monthlies and quarterlies, and of course, in the bumper holiday issues. I can say this without hesitation that he is the only modern writer in Bengali who has never wholly let me down. This is remarkable in an age of mushrooming literary reviews whose editors fling a deadline at you, coax you to write at the point of a gun, and sometimes even pay you well for it. The urge to compromise by dashing off trivia must be great. But Narendranath Mitra has not done so. This may be innate honesty or abundance of invention, or both. I like to think it is both.

Mahanagar was originally *Abataranika*, a "long short" which I read way back in 1955. I immediately, thought of turning it into a script. It would have been filmed then, right after *Pather Panchali,* if I had found a backer for it. But time was not ripe yet for a story that questioned traditional middle-class values, offered no romance, and no opportunities

Lobby card of *Mahanagar*

for songs or high dramatics. I finally made it in 1963. There are inevitable modifications in the film version — as those who know it will note — but most of the material and all of the inspiration came from the original story.

I am glad this translation has come out. I hope it will win new admirers for a writer of rare sensitivity and honesty.

LETTER ON RITWIK GHATAK'S AMAR LENIN

When Censor Board raised objections in granting Clearance certificate to Ritwik Ghatak's documentary film *Amar Lenin*, Ray wrote this letter to the producer of the film Sushil Karan disapproving the decision. Published in *Chitravas* Satyajit Ray Special Number, 1992

1/1 Bishop Lefroy Road, Calcutta 20   August 17, 1970

Shri Sushil Karan
Sumana Films, Calcutta

Dear Shri Karan,

I should like to thank you for arranging to show the documentary film *Amar Lenin* produced by you under the banner of Sumana Films.

I understand there has been some trouble in getting the film passed by the censors. This I find surprising, to put it mildly. I see nothing objectionable in either the subject matter or the treatment of it. I hope the authorities concerned will give the matter further thought, and revise their opinion of it, so that the film gets the necessary 'Certificate for Exhibition.'

Thanking you,

Yours sincerely
Satyajit Ray

Satyajit Ray

1/1 Bishop Lefroy Road, Calcutta - 20.   August 17, 1970

Shri Sushil Karan,
Sumana Films, Calcutta

Dear Shri Karan,

I should like to thank you for arranging to show the documentary film _Amar Lenin_ produced by you under the banner of Sumana Films.

I understand there has been some trouble in getting the film passed by the Censors. This I am find surprising, to put it mildly. I see nothing objectionable in either the subject matter or the treatment of it. I hope the authorities concerned will give the matter further thought, & revise their opinion of it, so that the film gets the necessary certificate for exhibition.

Thanking you again,

Yours sincerely,

Satyajit Ray

The facsimile of the letter written to Sushil Karan of Sumana Films by Ray dated 17.08.70

PRATIDWANDI

Foreword to *Pratidwandi* by Sunil Gangopadhyay, translated by Enakshi Chatterjee, Sangam Books, Delhi, 1974

As often as I am pressed into reading stories which I am assured — often erroneously — "would make wonderful films", I am asked why I chose this or that literary work for filming. "What drew you to it? What did you find in it that made you want to turn it into a screenplay?" "What do you look for in a story?"

Such questions are not easy to answer either briefly or with precision, because not one, not even a few, but a whole complex of reasons may account for one's settling for a particular work in preference to others. Theme, character, plot, incident, milieu, period — any or all of these may set up sympathetic vibrations of a sort that cannot be put into words, but can add up to the promise of a satisfying cinematic whole.

Still from *Pratidwandi*

I happened upon *Pratidwandi* at a time when I was looking not just for any suitable subject, but for a subject of a specific type. This was early in 1970. The urban scene was then dominated by the youth — whether in politics, on the fringe of it, or out of it. Joblessness, cynicism, the clash of generations, seething discontent exploding

Newspaper advertisement of *Pratidwandi* designed by Ray

into violence … one couldn't help reacting to it all and, going one step further, wishing to put some of this into a film. It was Sunil Ganguly's *Pratidwandi* which provided the springboard to turn the wish into reality.

I should put Sunil Ganguly high among present-day writers whom film-makers could read with profit. For one thing, he is a very visual writer. Characters, incidents, relationships are all largely built up by means of sensitively observed external details — a fundamentally cinematic device. The dialogue is sparse and life-like, with not a trace of high-falutin didacticism. If the surface appears simple, there is depth and density underneath; and there is lyricism too — for Sunil is a poet — to set beside the sudden, bold, wrenching scenes which strike one as much by their unexpectedness as by their conviction.

In *Pratidwandi* one finds all these qualities, given point and cohesion by the central character of Siddhartha, so endearing and believable in his contradictions, set by turns against his family, his friends, the girl he takes a fancy to, and the society which ultimately drives him to take refuge in a small job in a small town. If I were asked to give just one good reason for choosing this literary work, I would say it was Siddhartha.

CHITRABANI

Foreword to *Chitrabani*, Gaston Roberge, Kolkata, 1974

Gaston Roberge has written a film book which is aimed primarily at the Indian student of the cinema. Even ten years ago, a project like this would have made no sense. That it does so now is due to the enormous increase in interest in the cinema among the young people of the country, thanks largely to the spread of the film society movement. But this is not a phenomenon restricted to India alone. One has only to turn to the bibliography at the end of the book to realize what a vast amount of literature on the cinema is available to the enthusiast now. In my youth, when I set out in the pursuit of films, there were hardly a dozen worthwhile books on the subject in English. For aesthetics, one turned to Arnheim, to Spottiswoode, to Balasz and to Pudovkin. Eisenstein's erudite essays didn't see the light of day until the late forties. For history, there was Rotha, Bardèche and Brasillach, and if one's special interest lay in Hollywood, there was Lewis Jacobs. There were also a few odd collections of film criticisms — Agate's, C.A. Lejeune's, and a compilation by Alistair Cook called *Garbo and the Nightwatchman*. As for screenplays, one looked around in vain for them. The only film script in book form that I was able to track down was of Rene Clair's first English language film, *The Ghost Goes West*.

The situation has, of course, changed drastically. Today it is not unusual for even a modest pavement book stall in Calcutta or Bombay to display titles in the Cinema One series, or some of the admirable Lorrimer screenplays, or even a dog-eared old copy of *Cahiers du Cinema*. And the amazing thing is that these books and magazines don't stay in the stalls for long, but are picked up by young film buffs who are slowly building up their own private libraries.

Making his way through the cinematic maze, Gaston Roberge displays admirable patience, eclecticism and clear-headedness. Wisely, for a book of this nature, he takes nothing for granted. Even basic concepts like art and language and communication are freshly defined and related to the cinema in the particular context of India. Talking of drama, Roberge not only brings in Aristotle, but also the *Natya Shastra*, making an illuminating distinction between the Greek and the Indian points of view. Wherever possible, illustrative examples are provided to drive home an aesthetic or technical point. An especially useful section of the book towards the end gives a chronological listing of important foreign and Indian films since the inception of the cinema, and these are in turn related to concurrent artistic and social landmarks.

The whole book, indeed, is a labour of love, and I sincerely hope it will serve the purpose it is aimed at — to disseminate film culture and to promote a lively interest in the cinema, not only among young Indian cineastes, but also among the not-so-young ones.

One of the first things one notes about Roberge's book is its comprehensiveness. This is no easy matter when one thinks of the way the cinema has proliferated into a myriad branches and sub-branches. In our time we knew only of two categories: the professional commercial movie and the amateur home movie. The first (which included documentaries and newsreels) we paid money to see; the second didn't come our way at all unless we made them ourselves. The few avant-garde experiments abroad — Bunuel's, Cocteau's, Dulac's, and the 16 mm essays of *Maya Deren* — were almost like freaks which one took cognizance of but rarely thought of as trendsetters. Both Bunuel and Cocteau finally made the transition to a bigger market. But while they retained some of their idiosyncrasies even in their commercial films, experiment as such, on any considerable scale, disappeared from the cinema by the forties. It is only in the last two decades that it has returned, and on a scale large enough to deserve the appellation of a major trend. Indeed, what with all the frantic subterranean substandard activity in the USA and France, in Germany and Japan and Scandinavia, it is a moot question whether the new cinema — call it avant-garde or experimental or iconoclastic — does not outstrip in quantity the cinema of the conventional commercial type.

Ray with Gaston Roberge

It is also highly significant that the present book can talk of a traditional cinema as well as a modern one. This is a distinction which didn't exist 15 years ago, in the pre-Godard era. We believed a film was either good or bad. We didn't think of it in terms of being old-fashioned or modern. Chaplin was praised for his courage in using the silent technique in *Modern Times*. Modern critical opinion would surely have dubbed him retrograde.

All of which goes to make a global film scene of bewildering complexity. Conflicts and cross-currents abound; fashions are rampant; taboos and tenets by the dozen are being daily questioned and demolished; norms and styles and tastes are changing and evolving. Film-makers, entrepreneurs, critics and educators are floundering in an effort to keep on their feet on a shifting ground.

RAJASTHAN: INDIA'S ENCHANTED LAND

Foreword to *Rajasthan: India's Enchanted Land,* Raghubir Singh,
Thames and Hudson, London, 1981

When we were very young, a Bengali book we were much taken with was called *Rajkahini*, or Princely Tales. The tales were about real kings and real princes; but so filled were they with the stuff of romance and chivalry that they didn't seem real. We read of a land of desert and forest and mountain fastnesses; of marble palaces rising out of lakes like gem-studded lotuses; of brave Hindu warriors on faithful, fearless steeds charging into battle against invaders; and of their womenfolk who threw themselves into the flames rather than be snatched away as prizes by alien conquerors.

Rajasthan, whence these tales emerged, was known as Rajputana. I still prefer the four syllables to the three; they seemed magically to evoke a faraway, fairy-tale land. We looked at the map of India, and it only confirmed this feeling of remoteness. If Sind and Gujarat on the western tip formed the upper and lower jaws of the legless lion that held Kutch between its teeth, then Rajputana was its cheek, and Bengal, set well towards the eastern edge, was its slender waist. The Bengal we knew then was mostly flat and green and wet, while the Rajputana we read about was rugged and sunbaked and beautiful. Bengal had all the big rivers, but didn't have the Thar desert; and without a desert you couldn't have simoons and mirages and camel caravans trudging their way across endless sandy wastes. Also, Bengal had nothing in its past to compare with the procession of brave kings and stirring battles that marked the thousand-year history of Rajasthan. What was Plassey compared with Haldighat? And where were our heroes to set beside Prithviraj and Rana Pratap and Jai Singh?

I doubt if I'd have ever got to know Rajasthan well if I hadn't decided to become a film-maker. As a student of painting in Santiniketan, I had already discovered the exquisite world of Rajput miniatures, and realized that it wasn't just the martial arts that the Rajputs excelled in. And, of course, even as a child I knew some of the beautiful devotional songs of Mira, the Queen of Chittor, who shed her finery to become a lifelong devotee of Krishna. Indeed, the lure of the enchanted land had grown over the years, and as soon as I found an opportunity I decided to go filming in Rajasthan.

Although filming brings one closer to a place and its people — and I've been to Rajasthan six times — proximity has done nothing to dispel the aura that the place once held for me. If anything, by making me aware of its richness and diversity, it has entrenched itself even more deeply in my imagination.

Setting off from Jaipur by train and heading west, one notices how the land dips and rises by turns, how the wheat fields give way to scrubland, and the lush green to tawny ruggedness. At every halt in the journey, one observes the people. A very special breed, the men, proud in their whiskers and their turbans and their tunics flared at the waist. As one moves on westward, one watches the whiskers growing more luxurious, the turbans bigger and redder, the tunics shorter and more flamboyantly flared. The impression of strangeness is heightened by the delighted discovery, early on, that the ubiquitous and prosaic crows and sparrows of Bengal have all but disappeared, and their places taken by stately peacocks and fleet-winged green parakeets.

The contrasts are enough to take one's breath away. In a country where for miles one sees nothing but sand and rock and bramble and camels, I have seen a seven-mile stretch of marshland where thousands of birds from across the continents come and make their seasonal homes on treetops and tiny islets, filling the air with their calls and spattering the landscape with colour. I have seen fortresses perched on hilltops, fortresses rising out of barren plains, fortresses in forests, fortresses in the middle of cities and fortresses nestling in the lap of mountains. I have seen palaces and havelis of marble and stone, airy ones and massive ones, all with exquisite carvings on them; and I have seen the ruins of a village of stone dwellings which go back a thousand years. In the museums I have seen swords and shields and lances the warrior kings fought with, some studded with jewels, all impeccably crafted; and I have seen paintings on the walls of present-day dwellings where the colours and brushwork strike one dumb by their sweep and gaiety. And, of course, the women — and this goes for the whole of Rajasthan — women stepping straight out of the miniatures, decked out in brilliant reds and greens and yellows, disporting themselves with a grace that would rouse a queen's envy, and striking a joyous note in the drabbest of surroundings.

And music, too. The strangely beautiful bowed instrument with a tinkling bell, the ravanhatta, that the man in the blue tunic played all along the way as we rode on a caparisoned elephant up the ramp to the Amber Palace. Then, at the end of a day's hard work, the limpid melody on the double-flute that came floating over the horde of squatting camels we'd used earlier for our shooting, drawing us irresistibly to the dreamy-eyed Moslem who played it, and who regaled us with many more such melodies. I shan't forget, either, the old, bearded Moslem in Jaisalmer, desperately poor, who sang lovingly filigreed classical ragas, sitting in our hotel room, while he ran a bow vigorously across a kind of sarengi I'd never seen before.

It is no surprise that a segment of India which has inspired poets and painters, novelists and playwrights (Bengal alone provides many examples) should also inspire the photographer. More so because there are few places as photogenic as Rajasthan. Raghubir Singh himself belongs to Rajasthan, and hence knows its soils and seasons. This might well have worked against him, depriving him of the objectivity and freshness of viewpoint that an outsider can bring to bear on a place and its people. One notes with delight that this has not happened in the present case. Raghubir's view of Rajasthan in all its varied aspects, from the most mundane to the most splendorous, reveals a mixture of wonder, admiration and probing curiosity which, added, to his skill and experience as a craftsman, gives this album of photographs a very special distinction.

BRIEF ENCOUNTERS

Foreword to *Brief Encounters* by Amita Malik, New Delhi, 1982

Amita Malik, whom I have known as Amy for close on thirty years, has displayed an unwavering devotion to cinema ever since she emerged as a film critic in the early fifties. Living mostly in Delhi, she has pursued films not only at home, but also at major international film festivals abroad — in Berlin, Cannes, Venice, Moscow — occasionally making forays into other regions where local film personalities have yielded to her persuasion and obliged her with their views on their profession.

At festivals, Amy has not only written up films she has consumed with a ravenous appetite, she has also found time to waylay attending luminaries and record their observations for posterity. The present collection, covering a period of about twenty-five years, consists almost entirely of such interviews.

As the very name of the book suggests, these are not extended in-depth probes yielding profound revelations. Rather, these are pieces of journalism, terse and eclectic, which afford a glimpse into the minds of some of the best known names in world cinema. That Amy's curiosity ranges wide is clearly in evidence. Such Hollywood greats as Hitchcock, James Stewart and Peter Sellers are coaxed into airing their views along with master film-makers like Bergman, De Sica, Kurosawa and Antonioni, and Third World figures like Littin, Solans, Torre-Nilsson and Sembene. Cheek by jowl with these are some of our own stars — today's and yesterday's — Sharmila Tagore, Raj Kapoor, Dilip Kumar, Meena Kumari, Kanan Devi.

Amita Malik in conversation with Ray
and Marlon Brando, 1967

As one making films for over twenty-five years, I have grown a bit blasé about critical observation on films — my own films as well as others' — but I have a ready ear for what film people have to say about their own work. I have enjoyed listening to them in this book, as I'm sure many others will. Incidentally, *Brief Encounters* is the first book of its kind to be published in India. All the more reason why it should be welcomed by the growing body of film lovers in our country.

THE APU TRILOGY

Preface to *The Apu Trilogy*, translated by Shampa Banerjee, Seagull Books, Kolkata, 1985

The Apu Trilogy was not conceived as a trilogy. When we made *Pather Panchali* ["Song of the Road"], we couldn't think beyond the film. The critical and box office success of *Pather Panchali* triggered off *Aparajito* ["The Unvanquished"], which flopped and left me confused as to what I should do next. I made two contrasting films — *Parash Pathar* and *Jalsaghar* ["The Music Room"] — by which time *Aparajito* had gone on to win the top prize at the Venice film festival. It was at the press conference in Venice that I was asked if I had a trilogy in mind. I found myself saying yes. At that time I didn't know if there was a third film in Bibhutibhushan's novel. I came back home, reread *Aparajito*, and discovered *Apur Sansar* ["The World of Apu"] in it.

Both *Pather Panchali* and *Aparajito* are largely the work of amateurs as far as the externals of technique are concerned. Both films came to inordinate lengths when first edited, and had to be whittled down, sometimes leading to the omission of entire scenes. By the time of *Apur Sansar*, we had acquired a certain amount of professional competence. The script here was tighter, and so was the shooting. As a result, nothing was found to be redundant at the time of cutting.

All three films of the trilogy have long stretches of silence. This called for a greater amount of background music than is normally required. Two sequences in *Pather Panchali*, both virtually wordless, were conceived in terms of music. One was the sequence of the rain, and the other the long episode with Apu following the death of Durga. For the first, Ravi

Shankar provided a three-minute piece on the solo sitar in a raga which is conventionally associated with rain — Desh. For the sombre passage following Durga's death, the raga chosen was Todi.

Music also played a crucial part in the scene where Sarbojaya's pent-up feelings are released in a flood of tears as Harihar shows her the sari he has brought for Durga. Here, instead of the sound of weeping, we hear the dilruba's soulful lament in the upper reaches of the raga Patdeep.

The main theme of *Pather Panchali*, usually heard on the bamboo flute, evolved in Ravi Shankar's mind even before he had seen the film. It was certainly a stroke of inspiration. Also inspired are certain musical motifs in the other two films. The raga Jog is the basis of the melody which is heard in an impassioned outburst upon the death of Harihar in *Aparajito*. The same motif serves to suggest Sarbojaya's loneliness in the later stages of the film. Similarly inspired is the use of the poignant raga Lachari Todi in *Apur Sansar* to represent the Apu–Aparna relationship.

There is one scene in *Apur Sansar* which is crucial from the point of view of music. It shows Apu's aimless wanderings after Aparna's death, and ends with him throwing away the manuscript of his novel in a gesture of renunciation. The music here, scored for flute and strings, has the noble simplicity of a vedic hymn.

RABINDRANATH TAGORE: A CELEBRATION OF HIS LIFE AND WORK

Introduction to *Rabindranath Tagore: A Celebration of His Life and Work*, edited by
Ray Monk and Andrew Robinson, Rabindranath Tagore Festival Committee,
London & MoMA, Oxford, 1986

Rabindranath Tagore's complete works run to twenty-six volumes, and they do not include his letters, there are about twenty volumes of these, and more are coming out. Naturally, there is a great deal of Tagore which I have not read. As a poet, dramatist, novelist, short story writer, essayist, painter, song composer, philosopher and educationist Tagore was exceptionally versatile. But with indifferent translations Tagore will never be understood in the West as he is in Bengal. As a Bengali I know that as a composer of songs, he has no equal, not even in the West — and I know Schubert and Hugo Wolf; as a poet, he shows incredible felicity, range and development; some of his short stories are among the best ever written; his essays show an amazing clarity of thought and breadth of vision; in his novels he tackled some major themes and created some memorable characters; as a painter starting at the age of nearly seventy he remains, among the most original and interesting India has produced.

THE SELECT NONSENSE OF SUKUMAR RAY

Foreword to *The Select Nonsense of Sukumar Ray*, translated by Sukanta Chaudhuri, Oxford University Press, 1987

Portrait of Sukumar Ray drawn by Ray

S ukanta Chaudhuri asked me to write an introduction to his admirable translation of some of my father's nonsense verse and prose. I had already written a foreword in Bengali to a collected edition of my father's works, and it was later decided that Sukanta himself would translate this foreword and make it serve as an introduction to his book. The above is the result of his effort. Some passages which proved untranslatable have been left out. I had also made the remark that it was impossible to imagine *Ha-Ja-Ba-Ra-La* being translated into any other language. This too has been left out because Sukanta's very able and imaginative translation of this Carrollian fantasy is a refutation of my contention.

HENRI CARTIER-BRESSON IN INDIA

Foreword to *Henri Cartier-Bresson in India,* Thames and Hudson, London. 1987

The first Cartier-Bresson photographs I ever saw were in the French magazine *Verve*, way back in the thirties. They were, as far as I can recall, pictures of Mexico: a woman in black carrying a baby, a man with a haunted look in his eyes, with his arms around a sleeping boy. The credit said simply "Cartier" and I wasn't aware of the second half of the name, until in the early forties I came across a slim volume published by the Musuem of Modern Art, New York. This was a catalogue of photographs by Henri Cartier-Bresson. The double-barrelled version of the name had replaced the modest Cartier, but the photographs had the same compelling, mysterious and memorable quality, as distinctive and as instantly recognizable as the work of any great painter. Here was a new way of looking at things — the eye seeking the subject matter, and at the same time, it's most expressive disposition in

Picture postcard given to Ray by Cartier-Bresson

geometrical terms within the conventional rectangle of the photographic space. The style was unique in its fusion of head and heart, in its wit and its poetry. No one describes the method better than the master himself: "[Photography] is at one and the same time the recognition of a fact in a fraction of a second and the rigorous arrangement of the forms visually perceived which give the fact expression and significance."

I became an instant and lifelong aficionado of Cartier-Bresson. The first trip Cartier-Bresson made to India was in the late forties. At least I haven't seen any photographs dated earlier than 1947. It was probably the Partition which drew him to India, but he soon found himself confronted by a second major political event — the assassination of Mahatma Gandhi. This led to a series of memorable photographs of the funeral, especially remarkable for the way they eschewed sensualism.

Message from Cartier-Bresson to Ray written on the other side of the picture postcard

However, the majority of the Cartier-Bresson Indian photographs have nothing to do with political events. Most of them show ordinary people — in the streets, in the bazaars, by the riverside, up in the mountains — as individuals or in the mass — living their daily lives. The deep regard for people that is revealed in these Indian photographs as well as in his photographs of any people anywhere in the world, invests them with a palpable humanism. Add to this the unique skill and vision that raise the ordinary and the ephemeral to a monumental level, and you have the hallmark of the greatest photographer of our time.

CINEMA AND I

Foreword to *Cinema and I* by Ritwik Ghatak, Rupa & Co., Calcutta, 1987

In a career that spanned over twenty-five years until his death in 1976 at the age of fifty, Ritwik Ghatak left behind him eight feature films and a handful of unfinished fragments. Not a large output if one considers him only as a film-maker. But Ritwik was much more than just that. He was a film teacher, doing a stint as the vice-principal of the Film Institute at Pune; he was a playwright and producer, identifying himself with the Indian People's Theatre movement; he was also a writer of short stories, claiming that he wrote over fifty which were published, the earliest ones being written when he was barely out of his teens. Of these a dozen have been unearthed; the rest lie buried in the pages of obscure literary journals, many of which are probably defunct.

What has come as a surprise is the extent to which Ritwik wrote about the cinema. His Bengali articles number well over fifty and cover every possible aspect of the cinema. The present volume brings together his writings on the same subject in English.

Ritwik had the misfortune to be largely ignored by the Bengali film public in his lifetime. Only one of his films, *Meghe Dhaka Tara* (Cloud-capped Star), had been well received. The rest had brief runs, and generally lukewarm reception from professional film critics. This is particularly unfortunate, since Ritwik was one of the few truly original talents in the cinema this country has produced. Nearly all his films are marked by an intensity of feeling coupled with an imaginative grasp of the technique of film making. As a creator of powerful images in an epic style, he was virtually unsurpassed in Indian cinema. He

The book cover designed by Ray

also had full command over the all-important aspect of editing: long passages abound in his films which are strikingly original in the way they are put together. This is all the more remarkable when one doesn't notice any influence of other schools of film-making on his work. For him Hollywood might not have existed at all. The occasional echo of classical Soviet cinema is there, but this doesn't prevent him from being in a class by himself.

Ritwik's writings in English on the cinema relate to most aspects of his work. Some deal with personal attitude to film-making; some to the state of the cinema in the country; others are concerned with various aspects of film technique; yet others with his own individual films. When writing about his own works, one gets the impression that Ritwik was anxious to explicate them to his audience. One feels the artist's anxiety not to be misunderstood. He lays particular stress on aspects which are not obvious on the surface: such as what he derived from an early study of Jung — the use of the archetype, the Mother image and even the concept of rebirth.

Thematically, Ritwik's lifelong obsession was with the tragedy of Partition. He himself hailed from what was once East Bengal where he had deep roots. It is rarely that a director dwells so single-mindedly on the same theme. It only serves to underline the depth of his feeling for the subject.

I hope this book, which in its totality gives you a remarkably coherent self-portrait of the film-maker, will serve to heighten interest in his films which, after all, are the repository of all that he believed in as an artist and as a human being.

STORIES

Introduction to *Stories* by Satyajit Ray, Seagull Books, Calcutta, 1987

In 1913, my grandfather Upendrakishore Ray launched a children's monthly magazine called *Sandesh*. *Sandesh* is the name of a popular Bengali sweetmeat; but the word also means 'information'. Upendrakishore Ray had a formidable talent as a children's writer, having already published a delightful collection of Bengali folk tales as well as children's versions of the two famous Indian epics Ramayana and Mahabharata. All three were embellished with his own beautiful illustrations. The books and the magazine were published from his own press, U. Ray & Sons; my grandfather was a process engraver of the highest eminence.

Upendrakishore Ray died in 1915, six years before I was born. In the two years that he edited *Sandesh*, he filled its pages with stories, articles and illustrations. After his death, his eldest son, my father Sukumar Ray, took over. Sukumar Ray, too, had unique gifts as a children's writer and comic illustrator. Apart from school stories, plays and articles, he wrote a series of nonsense rhymes for the magazine which went on to win a permanent place in Bengali literature. *Sandesh* folded four years after my father's death. Soon, U. Ray Sons too closed down. My mother and I moved to my maternal uncle's house, where I grew up, finished my education and, in 1943, joined a British advertising agency as a junior visualizer. I had no literary bent at all, and never thought that I might one day write stories. What interested me besides advertising was films, although advertising seemed more dependable as a profession. I was in advertising for twelve years before I relinquished it to brave the hazards of a career in films.

It was in 1961, after I had established myself as a film-maker, that a poet friend of mine and I hit upon the idea of reviving *Sandesh*. The idea soon became a reality. The first issue of the revived *Sandesh* came out in the Bengali new year, in May 1961, on my fortieth birthday. As one of the two editors, I felt I had to contribute something. I produced a Bengali version of Edward Lear's *The Jumblies*. The second issue of *Sandesh* carried my first short story with my own illustration. Since then I have been writing and illustrating regularly for *Sandesh*, which celebrated its twenty-fifth anniversary this year.

Some of the stories I have written reflect my love of Verne and Wells and Conan Doyle whose works I read as a schoolboy. Professor Shonku, the scientist inventor, may be said to be a mild-mannered version of Professor Challenger, where the love of adventure takes him to remote corners of the globe. Four of his adventures are included here. I don't think the other stories in this volume show any marked influence. Among these are straightforward tales as well as tales of the fantastic and the supernatural for which I have a special fascination.

I enjoy writing stories for its own sake and derive a pleasure from it which is quite distinct from the pleasure of the vastly more intricate business of making a film. I have written stories both during the making of a film and in the free period — usually lasting about six months — between films.

Ray during the shooting of *Joy Baba Felunath*, 1978. Photograph by Sandip Ray

THE ADVENTURES OF FELUDA

Author's Note to *The Adventures of Feluda*, translated from Bengali by Chitrita Banerji, Penguin Books, 1988

I have been an avid reader of crime fiction for a very long time. I read all Sherlock Holmes stories while still at school. When I revived the children's magazine *Sandesh* which my grandfather launched seventy-five years ago, I started writing stories for it. The first Feluda story — a long short — appeared in 1965. Felu is the nickname of Pradosh Mitter, private investigator. The story was told in first person by Felu's Watson — his fourteen-year-old cousin Tapesh. The suffix "da" (short for "dada") means an elder brother.

Although the Feluda stories were written for the largely teenaged readers of *Sandesh*, I found they were being read by their parents as well. Soon longer stories followed — novelettes — taking place in a variety of picturesque settings. A third character was introduced early on: Lalmohan Ganguli, writer of cheap, popular thrillers. He serves as a foil to Felu and provides dollops of humour.

When I wrote my first Feluda story, I scarcely imagined he would prove so popular that I would be forced to write a Feluda novel every year. To write a whodunnit while keeping in mind a young readership is not an easy task, because the stories have to be kept "clean". No illicit love, no crime passionel, and only a modicum of violence. I hope adult readers will bear this in mind when reading these stories.

MUSIC CD OF JALSAGHAR

On Music CD of *Jalsaghar* by Ocora Radio, France, 1988

After the box office failure of my second film *Aparajito* (The Unvanquished), I was a little unsure as to what kind of film I should make next. After some deliberation, I decided on a film featuring singing and dancing — a formula which usually worked with the Indian audience. I chose a popular short story — *Jalsaghar* — about the last days of a music-loving feudal baron. The screenplay, however, developed into a serious study of decaying feudalism. The songs and dances were retained but became classical instead of popular. I was fortunate to be able to use some of the leading singers and instrumentalists for the film. As a composer, I chose the great sitar virtuoso Vilayat who was most ably assisted by his younger brother Imrat Khan, also a sitar virtuoso. The two of them provided superb solos and duets for the background music for which — with the exception of violins — only Indian instruments were used. All the background score is area-based. There is a great deal of music in the foreground too, but there is an attempt to weave it into the fabric of the plot.

I am extremely happy that a compact disc is being produced on the music of *Jalsaghar*.

LEGION OF HONOUR

Extract from acceptance speech for Legion of Honour (conferred upon him in 1987 by the French Government), Kolkata, 2 February, 1989

Ray receiving the honour from the French President François Mitterrand at Kolkata. Photograph by Nemai Ghosh, courtesy Satyaki Ghosh

Ladies and gentlemen, I feel immensely happy and proud to receive this very great honour from France in the year of the Festival of France and the two hundredth anniversary of the French Revolution. I would like to take this opportunity to acknowledge my debt to the French cinema. I have learnt a great deal from the films of the great French masters and I consider Jean Renoir as my principal mentor. At this signal honour I feel fulfilled as an Indian artist and I feel that my constant devotion to the art of the cinema over the years has not been in vain. Thank you.

THE CHESS PLAYERS AND OTHER SCREENPLAYS

Preface to *The Chess Players and Other Screenplays*, Faber and Faber, London, 1989

Of the three screenplays in this book, two — *The Chess Players* and *Deliverance* — are based on the short stories by the famous Urdu and Hindi writer Prem Chand. The third, *The Alien*, is an original screenplay by me. The three subjects could hardly be more disparate in style and content. *Deliverance*, which was made for the television, deals with Untouchability and is distinctly angry in tone. *The Chess Players*, which is about the annexation of an Indian native state by the British Raj, is quite often funny in spite of its weighty theme. It is also my most expensive film, whereas *Deliverance* cost very little money. *The Alien*, which was never filmed, is best described as a whimsy.

These primary reasons drew me to *The Chess Players*: my interest in chess, in the Raj period, and in the city of Lucknow where I spent many delightful holidays in my childhood and youth. It is the capital of Oudh, which was annexed by the then Governor-General of India, Lord Dalhousie. This was done through the agency of General Outram, who was the British political agent in Lucknow. Research revealed that the deposed King Wajid Ali Shah was an extraordinary character. Outram describes him as a worthless king, which he probably was, but this was compensated for by a genuine gift for music. He was a composer, singer, poet and dancer. He also wrote and produced plays on Hindu themes (he was a Muslim himself) in which he acted the main part. All this made the king a figure worthy of film treatment. As for the character of Outram, I was struck by the fact that he had qualms about the task he had been assigned to perform. This was revealed in a couple of Dalhousie's letters. Thus, both the king and Outram were complex, three-dimensional characters. Chess is used as a metaphor for the political manoeuvrings of the Raj as well as an actual ingredient of a subplot involving two noblemen, addicts of the game. The two friends, fearing trouble, retire into a village and play right through the Annexation and the arrival of the British army in Lucknow. Their story is treated in a light vein, although there is a note of pathos at the end.

I made *Deliverance* because I had been wanting to make a film about the poorest of the poor, something I had never done before. The dramatic aspect of the Brahmin–Untouchable confrontation is vividly conveyed by Prem Chand in his story. I found it replete with cinematic possibilities.

The Alien germinated from a short story I wrote for the magazine for young people which I have been editing for the last twenty-five years. It concerned a meek village schoolmaster whose life is changed by an extraordinary lucky encounter with an extraterrestrial. The idea of a supremely intelligent alien landing in a village where most of the inhabitants are unlettered was lodged in my mind for a long time as a possible film subject. In 1966, I met Arthur Clarke on a visit to London. Kubrick had then been filming 2001 from Clarke's story, and Clarke had actually come to meet Kubrick. Clarke took me to the studio where I met the director and watched some of the shooting. On the way back from the studio, in the car, I gave Clarke a brief idea of the kind of sci-fi film I had in mind. Clarke encouraged me, and later, after his return to Sri Lanka where he lived, told his partner Mike Wilson about *The Alien*, which is the title I had in mind for my film. Wilson was enthused enough to fly down to Calcutta and make me write the screenplay virtually at the point of a gun. The work was completed in a fortnight. Wilson immediately started to work on setting up the production. Soon I found myself in Hollywood where Columbia had read the screenplay and had provisionally agreed to finance it. But, like many a cherished project, *The Alien* never really got off the ground.

The Alien was meant to be a bilingual film where the Indian characters would speak in Bengali among themselves, and all scenes involving the American engineer would be spoken in English. The screenplay, however, was written entirely in English. What is printed here is the first draft that Columbia found acceptable.

THE ART OF RABINDRANATH TAGORE

Foreword to *The Art of Rabindranath Tagore* by Andrew Robinson,
Andre Deutsch, London, 1989

Rabindranath Tagore took to painting at a later stage in his life. Some manuscripts dating back to his youth show doodles in the margin which suggest a natural flair for drawing. After that there is nothing to show that he had any interest in visual expression until, when he was well over sixty, fantastic forms began to appear in his manuscripts. Where one would normally cross out a word or a sentence, Rabindranath turned them into grotesque creatures. These emendations were stung together until the whole page took on the appearance of a tapestry of words and images.

In time, paintings and calligraphic drawings began to appear as independent efforts, unrelated to manuscripts. Blue-black ink gave way to transparent colours, and the subjects became more and more varied. The output clearly suggests that Rabindranath was absorbed in his new pursuit and enjoying the experience. The lack of formal training was compensated by an instinctive feel for rhythm, texture and spacing. There was also the calligraphic virtuosity when he used the pen. (His unique and beautiful Bengali handwriting — which came to be known as the "Rabindrik" script — has been widely imitated.) But the brush, too, was frequently used. Some of the efforts were purely abstract, while others dealt with subjects which covered a wide field.

Except where human figures were concerned, Rabindranath's work remained rooted in fantasy. He painted flora and fauna which belonged to no known species. The landscapes often have a mood which suggests dusk in rural Bengal, but here too the trees cannot be identified. Flowers, birds, fish and animals in his paintings inhabit a world which belonged uniquely to Rabindranath. Sometimes a painting and a poem are combined, the former making a frame for the latter. Examples of this are to be found both in colour and black and white. Sometimes the sheet is filled with a frenzy of convoluted forms painted in iridescent colours. The mood evoked here is of a joyous freedom.

But Rabindranath's special field remained the study of women. These women are recognizably Bengali, portrayed in an infinity of moods and expressions. The lack of anatomical accuracy does not matter since, in the best examples, the total effect is haunting.

Rabindranath's paintings and drawings number well over two thousand. Considering the late start, this makes for an astonishing output of great fecundity. It is important to stress that he was uninfluenced by any painter, Eastern or Western. His work does not stem from any tradition but is truly original. Whether one likes it or not, one has to admit its uniqueness. Personally, I feel it occupies a place of major importance beside his equally formidable output of novels, short stories, plays, essays, letters and songs.

LETTER ON SAFDAR HASHMI

Published in the souvenir of Safdar Hashmi Memorial Committee, on the occasion of Safdar Hashmi Samaroh, 12–16 April, 1989

Dear Mrs. Hashmi,

I had been away in Bombay in connection with some work on a new film — hence the delay in replying.

Your letter greatly touched me. Although I never met your husband, nor ever seen any of his work, I now realise what a brave and talented person he was. I am fully in sympathy with what you are doing to perpetrate his memory.

That your husband produced a version of Goopy & Bagha on the stage came as a great and very pleasant surprise to me. You may be interested to know that I am now working on a third sequel to Goopy & Bagha just now.

I am enclosing a letter which I hope will serve as a message to Safdar Hashmi Samaroh.

With all best wishes,

Yours sincerely
Satyajit Ray

Dear Mr Hashmi,

I had been away in Bombay in connection with some work on a new film — hence the delay in replying.

Your letter greatly touched me. Although I never met your husband, nor ever seen any of his work, I now realize what a brave and talented person he was. I am fully in sympathy with what you are doing to perpetuate his memory.

That your husband produced a version of Goopy & Bagha on the stage came as a first & very pleasant surprise to me. You may be interested to know that I am now working on a third sequel to Goopy & Bagha just now.

I am enclosing a letter which I hope will serve as a message to SAFDAR HASHMI SAMAROH.

With all good wishes —

Yours sincerely,

The facsimile of the letter written to Mrs Hashmi by Ray

NAARI

Foreword to *Naari*, Calcutta Ladies Study Group, edited by Tilottama Tharoor, 1990

What were the women of Calcutta like when Charnock fortuitously founded the city? I am by no means a historian, but I have read some accounts by travellers from the West of life in India in the 17th century. I still don't know the answer. Almost inevitably, these travellers stress the horrors of "suttee" and the wretched plight of widows. Francois Bernier, who came here in the latter part of Shah-Jehan's rule, does the same, but at the same time acknowledges "the beauty and amiable disposition of the native Bengali women." I don't know if one can make assumptions from evidences of this nature, but from the many studies of Bengali women by Western artists visiting Bengal a couple of centuries earlier, it would seem that women — particularly of the rural class — led a less cloistered life in those days. Otherwise how could they go about their business by the pond while a Sahib sat by on a stool sketching them?

Serious and concerted efforts at emancipation of women didn't begin until the 19th century with the emergence of some great humanitarian reformers. Naturally, the centre of activity was Calcutta. Only one image will suffice to prove that it bore fruit:

The character sketch of Bimala from *Ghare Baire*, one of Ray's bold female protagonists

Booklet cover of *Mahanagar,* a film that centres around its female protagonist

Satyendranath Tagore and his wife cantering around the Maidan on horseback.

I have been brought up in an atmosphere totally free from the taints of superstition. When, as a child, I lost my father and moved to my uncle's house, my mother soon started to take a daily bus ride from the south to the far north of the city to teach in a school for widows. In fact, evidences of emancipation were all around me, but I was too young to understand. Today, in the rambunctious city that is Calcutta, women have caught up with men, the only difference left being physiological. Doubtless, the essays in this volume will deal with the various aspects of this change and growth.

I congratulate the Ladies Study Group on this very worthwhile undertaking.

SATYAJIT RAY AT 70

Preface to *Satyajit Ray at 70* by Nemai Ghosh, Orient Longman, 1990

Ray with his 'Boswell', Nemai Ghosh. Photograph by Satyaki Ghosh

For close on twenty-five years, Nemai Ghosh has been assiduously photographing me in action and repose — a sort of Boswell working with a camera rather than a pen. In so far as these pictures rise above mere records and assume a value as examples of a photographer's art, they are likely to be of interest to a discerning viewer. I hope Nemai's efforts will not go in vain.

THE OTHER RAY

Introduction to *The Other Ray: Illustrations, Graphic Design, Drawings and Sketches for Films by Satyajit Ray,* edited by Dolly Narang, The Village Gallery, New Delhi 1990

My grandfather was, among other things, a self-taught painter and illustrator of considerable skill and repute, and my father — also never trained as an artist — illustrated his inimitable nonsense rhymes in a way which can only be called inspired. It is, therefore, not surprising that I acquired the knack to draw at an early age. Although I trained for three years as a student of Kalabhavan in Santiniketan under Nandalal Bose, I never became a painter. Instead, I decided to become a commercial artist and joined an advertising agency in 1943, the year of the great Bengal famine. Not content with only one pursuit, I also became involved in book designing and typography for an enterprising new publishing house.

In time I realized that since an advertising agency was subservient to the demands of its clients, an advertising artist seldom enjoyed complete freedom.

This led me to the profession of film-making where, in the thirty-five years that I've been practising it, I have given expression to my ideas in a completely untrammelled fashion.

As is my habit, along with film-making, I have indulged in other pursuits which afford me the freedom I hold so dear. Thus, I have been editing a children's magazine for thirty years, writing stories for it and illustrating them, as well as illustrating stories by other writers.

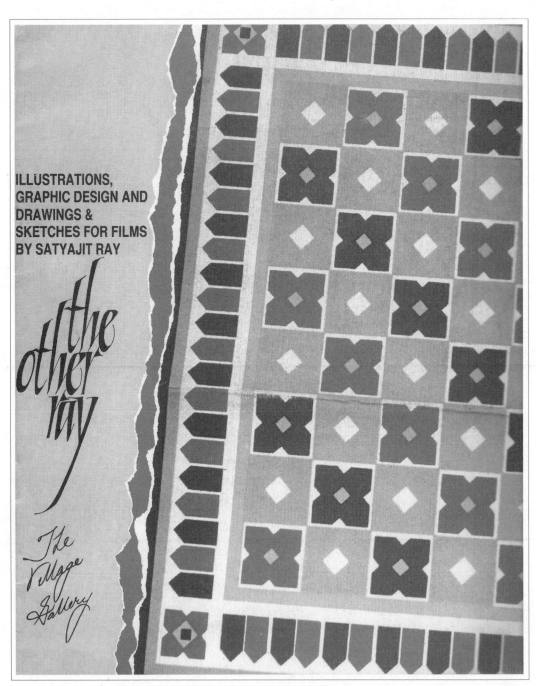

ILLUSTRATIONS,
GRAPHIC DESIGN AND
DRAWINGS &
SKETCHES FOR FILMS
BY SATYAJIT RAY

the other ray

The Village Gallery

The cover of the catalogue *The Other Ray*

Illustrations by Ray in the magazine *Sandesh* from the catalogue

While preparing a film, I've given vent to my graphic propensities by doing sketches for my shooting scripts, designing sets and costumes, and even designing posters for my own films.

Since I consider myself primarily to be a film-maker and, secondarily, to be a writer of stories for young people, I have never taken my graphic work seriously, and I certainly never considered it worthy of being exposed to the public. It is entirely due to the tenacity and persuasiveness of Mrs. Narang that some samples of my graphic work are now being displayed. Needless to say, I'm thankful to Mrs. Narang; but at the same time, I must insist that I do not make any large claims for them.

CALCUTTA: A HOMAGE

Calcutta: A Homage, Calcutta Tercentenary Steering Committee, 1992

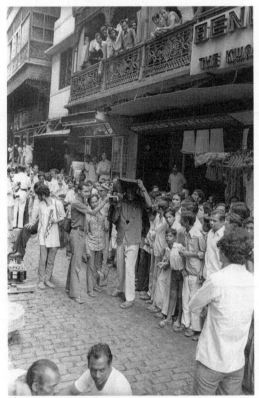

Ray shooting in the streets of Kolkata. Photograph by Nemai Ghosh, courtesy Satyaki Ghosh

Some of the leading foreign travel guides put Calcutta at the head of their lists of "Places to Avoid at all Costs". This may make our hackles rise, but the fact remains that in its physical aspect, Calcutta displays features to daunt the most intrepid of travellers. The mass of humanity that inhabits the city and is seemingly out on the streets en masse at all times of the day; the streets themselves, particularly the main thoroughfares, teeming with conglomerate traffic bumping over ubiquitous pot-holes while sweating thelawallas and rickshaw pullers — in themselves a shock to the unaccustomed eye — weave their perilous way through it; the architecture that is neither fish nor fowl, but a mish-mash of styles and periods — much of it jerry-built and in bad taste — which only serves to underline the

The Calcutta Tercentenary logo, designed by Ray

disparity between the haves and the have-nots that is a feature of the subcontinent … all this makes for an assault on the senses that almost justifies the denigration the city has suffered in recent years.

And yet we know that if an outsider, overcoming the initial shock, found time to probe beneath the forbidding facade, and reached out towards the human component, he would be astonished to discover the warmth, energy and creativity that mark a surprisingly large section of Calcutta's inhabitants at all levels of society.

While this primarily accounts for the Calcuttan's deep attachment to the city, it can also justifiably be seen as the legacy left by some of the greatest men of the country who were either born in Calcutta or made Calcutta their home during the last 100 years. These men left their mark in fields as diverse as politics and literature, science and religion, education and social reform.

LEARN PHOTOGRAPHY

Foreword to *Learn Photography*, Photographic Association of Dum Dum, Kolkata, 1980

The Photographic Association of Dum Dum has achieved a commendable first — certainly in India — by producing a textbook on photography for its members, as well as for the camera buffs among the public. The widespread interest in still photography is among the more notable phenomena of this age of technology. In spite of the many fool-proof equipments now available in the market, photography remains an art and craft to be studied. What a book teaches must necessarily be supplemented by practice, and by the use of one's intuition, but the usefulness of a well-written guide cannot be minimized.

I heartily commend the Association's enterprise, more so because it goes to show how such an organization can fruitfully expand its activities, thereby setting an example for others to follow.

HEART CARE CENTRE

Message for Heart Care Centre by Dr. K.B. Bakshi, 1990

Ray of Hope for the Heart

The logo designed by Ray

I heartily welcome the move to build a heart hospital which would cater to all kinds of patients — both rich and poor. I think the venture needs the support of all right-thinking people. Every little would help towards a cause which has the welfare of the community at heart. I give my unstinted support to it.

Ray with Kishore Kumar during the recording of *Ghare Baire,* 1984. Photograph by Sadanand

KISHORE KUMAR

From the documentary film *Zindagi Ek Safar* by Sandip Ray, 1989

He had a special screening for us (for *Door Gagan Ki Chhaon Mein*) and I thought it has some very interesting touches and a lot of pathos and he was quite happy with it himself. Well, actually I think I met Kishore first when he was courting my niece Ruma whom he eventually married and this must have been towards the end of 1940s or early 1950s, I don't exactly remember, and ever since then of course I have known him and have been very friendly and very warm towards each other. He was of course gifted with an incredible voice as a popular singer. As a singer of popular songs, he had no equal I think and I feel that even if he had learnt classical singing he would have excelled in it because his voice was so fluent, so mellifluous, and so flexible. So, there came a time when I needed him for one of my films. This was in 1963, I was making *Charulata* based on a Tagore short story and I needed a song in a male voice, to be sung by the hero. I approached Kishore and he only insisted on doing the recording in Bombay, he said he would prefer to do it in Bombay rather than in Calcutta, with his own recordists. Four or five years ago I wanted him again for one of my films, again a Tagore story — *Ghare Baire* (Home and the World) — and here I needed three songs, and again the recording was done in Bombay. But this time there was no accompaniment needed. One thing I forgot to mention and I think it's important to mention it to show what kind of a person Kishore was, and what sort of relationship he had with me is that both for *Charulata* where he sang one song, and for *Ghare Baire*, where he sang three songs, he did not charge any money, he did it for free.

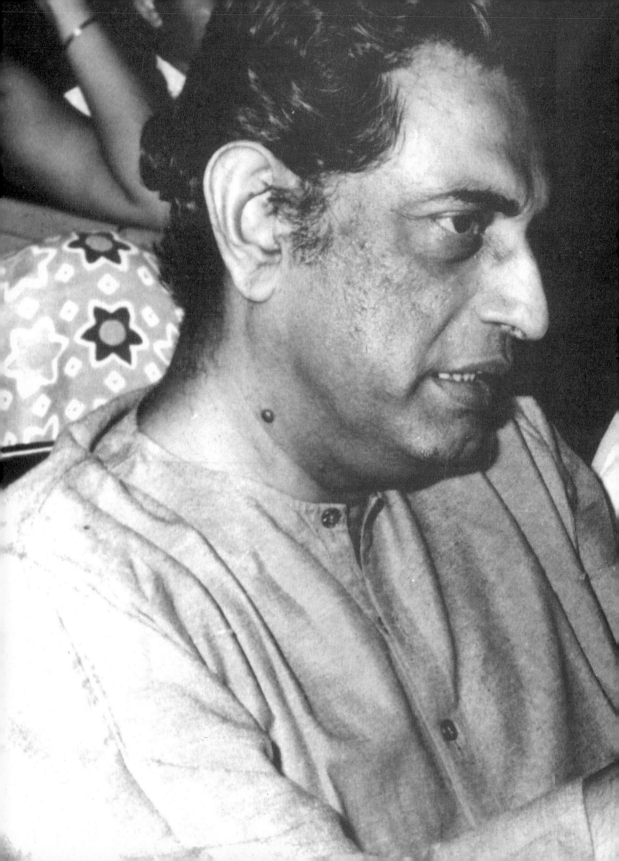

Ray with Kishore Kumar during a private film
show at the Ramnord Preview Theatre, Mumbai.
Photograph by Sadanand

MADHABI CHAKRABORTY

From the documentary film *Portrait of an Actress* by Shlla Datta, 1991

Poster of *Charulata* designed by Ray

I first saw Madhabi in Mrinal Sen's film *Baishe Shraban*. Before that I had seen pictures of her in film magazines, and seen that a new actress of promise, judging by the looks, had appeared on the screen and I was very keen to see her performance. Mrinal's film proved that she had quite a reserve of talent, and I offered her the leading role in my film *Mahanagar*. *Mahanagar* was a very demanding role. She was the wife of the hero. She was a mother, she was a daughter-in-law, she was a sister-in-law. Each facet required a different kind of performance and different kind of understanding of the role. And then after that she was a worker in a firm as a saleswoman. She had to contend with her boss, and she had friends among her co-workers. So, it was a very demanding, complicated, complex role. But I had no difficulty with her

A still from *Charulata*

because she was so intelligent and so quick on the uptake that she needed only very little guidance from me and was able to do the rest by herself.

After *Mahanagar* came *Charulata,* which many consider my best film, where she played the central role. It was based on Rabindranath's "Nastanirh" and she played the role of Charu. By now she was a more mature actress and I had even less difficulty with her. I don't think she ever required a second take or a third take; it was mostly the first take that was OK, and she scored absolutely heavily with her performance in the film. This was followed by a third film, *Kapurush,* which was also a very elegant film, with a very nice story, with a very demanding part for her. These are the three films where I worked with her. Later on I didn't have her in any of my films, but the memory of the three films is still fresh in my mind, and I hope this bears testimony to the excellence of Madhabi Chakraborty as an actress.

V. G. JOG

From *Sadhana* — a documentary on V. G. Jog by Ambrish Sangal, 1990

I can't quite recall when I met Jog ji for the first time. Well, I have the feeling that I have known him all my life. I have admired him for a long time for his performances as a soloist, and I have admired his jugalbandis with great musicians like Faiyaz Khan and Bade Ghulam Ali Khan and Bismillah Khan. He plays an instrument which is Western in origin — the violin — but which has proved eminently suited to our classical music. Actually, the violin was being used more in South India than elsewhere. But thanks to Jog ji, now it is being used in other parts of India as well. For his personal use, and I think the eventual use by others also, a new kind of violin has been made in Paris, which produces a sound — sort of a cross between a violin and a sarangi — so it's even more suited to Indian classical music than the older, the other kind of violin. Jog ji is a person of great charm and humility, which is one more reason why I have such high regard for him. I hope he will continue to be a star in the firmament of our musical life in India for a long time to come.

ACKNOWLEDGEMENTS

Lolita Ray
Souradeep Ray
Prasad Ranjan Ray
Jyotiprakash Mitra
Satyaki Ghosh
Arup K. De
Indrani Majumdar
Biswajit Mitra
Sourit Dey
Debajyoti Guha
Dibyendu Ash
Sarbajit Mitra
Rajib Chakraborty
Late Kaushik Ghosh
Binita Roy
Neeraj Nath

We acknowledge all the newspapers, periodicals, books and documentaries in which these pieces first appeared.

SOCIETY FOR THE PRESERVATION OF SATYAJIT RAY ARCHIVES

PRESERVING A PRICELESS LEGACY

Sometime after the demise of Satyajit Ray, a number of actors and public personalities—Amitabh Bachchan and the late Ismail Merchant being among them—teamed up to form what is today the Society for the Preservation of Satyajit Ray Archives. Popularly known as Satyajit Ray Society, it was founded in 1994 with the objective of restoring and preserving the priceless legacies left by the master director as also of disseminating his work worldwide.

RAY RESTORATION

When Ray breathed his last in 1992, negatives and prints of many of his films, especially those of his early classics, were in a precarious state. David H. Shepard, a noted film preservationist in California, came to India to examine the original negatives of the Ray films. He found the negatives of 18 of his films in 'tatters'. Restoration of Ray films was the Society's primary concern at the time. It went into a tie-up with the Los Angeles based Academy of Motion Picture Arts and Sciences, the hallowed institution which had conferred the Oscar for Lifetime Achievement on Ray. So far, a large number of the maestro's thirty-six film-oeuvre has been restored at the Academy Archive.

RAY ARCHIVES

Apart from his films, Ray left behind an astonishingly wide artistic universe comprising scripts, storyboards, posters, set, costume and book jacket designs, literary manuscripts, illustrations, music notations, advertisement artworks and so on. The Society has arguably the largest and most authentic archive on Ray in its custody. A veritable treasure trove, the Ray paper archive contains almost the entire creative output of his many-faceted genius. A large part of Ray's paper legacy was restored under the supervision of Mike Wheeler, Senior Conservator (Paper Preservation) at the Victoria-Albert Museum, London, and is housed in Ray's family home in Kolkata. The large personal library that Ray left and his personal effects are also being carefully preserved.

PUBLISHING RAY BOOKS

As part of the dissemination campaign, the Society has begun to publish books by Ray. It brought out *Deep Focus: Reflection on Cinema*, a collection of long-lost essays by Ray, in December 2011 in collaboration with HarperCollins India. The Society published, jointly with HarperCollins India, *Satyajit Ray's Ravi Shankar*, a facsimile edition of the visual script that the master director drew for his intended film on the sitar maestro. The Society also brought out *Probandho Sangroho*, a collection of Bengali essays by Ray, jointly with Ananda Publishers Pvt. Ltd. on 1 May 2015. Next, the Society brought out yet another book in collaboration with HarperCollins India—*The Pather Panchali Sketchbook*, which is a facsimile of the visual storyboard that Ray created for his maiden film. The last publication, which too is the outcome of the joint collaboration between the Society and HarperCollins India, is *Travails with the Alien*. The book includes Ray's script for *The Alien*, a film which he wanted to make in Hollywood but failed to do. The book was launched by Sharmila Tagore at a ceremony that the Society organized on 28 April 2018 to mark the ninety-seventh birth anniversary of Satyajit Ray. Now the Ray Society has tied up with Penguin Random House India to create the "Penguin Ray Library" which will strive to bring out the entire oeuvre of writings created by the master. Satyajit Ray has a long association with Penguin India and the coming together of the Society with Penguin Random House is a homecoming of sorts.

RAY MEMORIAL LECTURES

The Society has been organizing lectures dedicated to Ray's memory by distinguished film personalities for quite a few years. Javed Akhtar gave the first lecture in 2009, followed by Shyam Benegal (2012) and Naseeruddin Shah (2014). Soumitra Chatterjee delivered the next lecture on the eve of Ray's ninety-fourth birth anniversary on 1 May 2015, and Aparna Sen on 1 May 2017. Sharmila Tagore delivered the lecture on 28 April 2018. In 2019, Penguin Random House India collaborated with the society to create the Annual Penguin Ray Lecture Series. On that occasion, Tarun Majumdar gave a lecture on 27 April 2019.

EXHIBITIONS, SEMINARS AND FILM SHOWS

The Society has arranged quite a number of exhibitions of Ray's artworks as also festivals of his films and seminars on his work, at home and abroad. Some of the places where such shows and film retrospectives have taken place are Kolkata, Mumbai, Delhi, Hyderabad, Bangalore, Toronto, Valladolid, San Francisco, London and Amsterdam. The Society organized its largest seminar (on *Pather Panchali*) in August 2015 in Kolkata. The participants were Sharmila Tagore, Aparna Sen, Dibakar Banerjee, Shoojit Sircar, Nandita Das, Sujoy Ghosh, Suman Mukhopadhyay and Dileep Padgaonkar. The seminar was moderated by Dhritiman Chaterji. In 2019, the society organized an exhibition to commemorate 50 years of *Goopy Gyne Bagha Byne* at Kolkata.

www.satyajitrayworld.org / Email: satyajitraysociety@gmail.com